KHOONI VAISAKHI

NANAK SINGH (1897-1971) is widely regarded as the father of the Punjabi novel. With little formal education beyond the fourth grade, he wrote an astounding fifty-nine books, which included thirty-eight novels and an assortment of plays, short stories, poems, essays and even a set of translations. He received the Sahitya Akademi Award in 1962 for *Ik Myan Do Talwaraan*. His novel *Pavitra Paapi* was made into a film in 1968, while *Chitta Lahu* was translated into Russian by Natasha Tolstoy.

NAVDEEP SURI joined the Indian Foreign Service in 1983 and has served in India's diplomatic missions in Cairo, Damascus, Washington, Dar es Salaam and London and as India's Consul General in Johannesburg. He was India's High Commissioner to Australia and Ambassador to Egypt prior to his current assignment as Ambassador to UAE. He has translated into English his grandfather Nanak Singh's classic Punjabi novels *Pavitra Paapi* (as *The Watchmaker*) and *Adh Khidya Phul* (as *A Life Incomplete*).

KHOONI VAISAKHI

A POEM FROM THE
JALLIANWALA BAGH MASSACRE
1919

···

NANAK SINGH

TRANSLATED FROM THE PUNJABI BY
NAVDEEP SURI

HARPERPERENNIAL

First published in hardback in India in 2019 by Harper Perennial
An Imprint of HarperCollins *Publishers*
A-75, Sector 57, Noida, Uttar Pradesh 201301, India
www.harpercollins.co.in

2 4 6 8 10 9 7 5 3 1

Originally published as *Khooni Vaisakhi*, 1920
English Translation Copyright © Navdeep Suri 2019

'The Bagh, the Book and Our Bauji' Copyright © Navdeep Suri, 2019
'The Sins of the Great-Grandfather' Copyright © Justin Rowlatt, 2019
'Khooni Vaisakhi: A Historical and Humanistic Peresppective'
Copyright © H.S. Bhatia, Gajinder Bagga, 2019

P-ISBN: 978-93-5302-938-8
E-ISBN: 978-93-5302-939-5

Typeset in 10.5/15 Gentium Book at
Manipal Digital Systems, Manipal

Printed and bound at
Thomson Press (India) Ltd

CONTENTS

PREFACE

I had thought of translating my grandfather Nanak Singh's long poem *Khooni Vaisakhi* a few years back. I had completed translating his novel *Adh Khidya Phul* (*A Life Incomplete*) around the time, and was awaiting its publication. I took a cursory look at the poem, played around with a few verses in my head and gave up. Translating verse from Punjabi into English just wasn't my cup of tea, I decided. I should stick to prose.

But I was piqued by the fact that *Khooni Vaisakhi* wasn't just another one of his many books. It stemmed from a deep personal experience and was spot on with its historical references. Looking at some of his novels that were similarly rooted in real events, I zeroed in on *Ik Myan Do Talwaran*. This was the book that won him the Sahitya Akademi Award in 1962 and it was a story based around the martyrdom of Kartar Singh Sarabha and the famous Ghadar movement which saw an improbable group of young Indian nationalists in Vancouver and San Francisco coordinate with like-minded patriots from India in an abortive attempt to overthrow the British Raj in India. I was struck by the amount of research that the author had done to put together a truly memorable narrative. I started work on its translation and had made fair headway when the unfinished work met with an unusual accident. I had been posted as ambassador to Egypt and was diligently preparing for the move from Delhi. Among the hundreds of chores involved in the move was the relatively mundane task of copying all my personal files from the office laptop on to different pen drives before cleaning up the laptop, emptying its trash bin and returning it to office. One of these files was the incomplete translation of *Ik Myan* which I had planned to continue after settling down in Cairo. To my horror, the file that I copied was an old version that basically had the book's foreword and little else. I contacted my cousin Simar, an IT pro, to see if he could retrieve the deleted files from the laptop. His verdict: I had been a bit too diligent in cleaning up the computer. The files were beyond retrieval and there was nothing to do but to rue my own ineptitude.

And to take a break from translation. The last few years were also a blur in terms of the pressure of work and the disruptive effect of consecutive moves from Cairo to Canberra to Abu Dhabi and it wasn't until the middle of 2018 that the thought of translating *Khooni Vaisakhi* came up again during a visit to Amritsar. This time, it was in the context of a conversation with my parents about the upcoming centenary of the Jallianwala Bagh massacre in 2019 and the importance of taking *Khooni Vaisakhi* to a wider audience. Despite my reservations about translating verse, I decided to take up the project in earnest. But first, I would have to teach myself a thing or two about translating poetry.

Some years ago, at the Jaipur Literature Festival, I had attended a session where author–diplomat Pavan Varma and renowned poet Gulzar produced a delightful jugalbandi. In his uniquely mellifluous baritone, Gulzar would read one of his less-known poems in Hindi and Pavan would read a fluent English translation of the same poem from his book *Neglected Poems*. Gulzar had also graciously joined me at the launch of *A Life Incomplete* at the same festival in January 2012 and his generous compliment to Pavan that in some of the poems, the translation read better than his original stuck in my head. I had bought a copy of *Neglected Poems* and I now dove into it with a sense of purpose, hoping perhaps to find the magic key that would help me unlock *Khooni Vaisakhi*. It is a beautiful book of translation, but I found nothing that I could connect with my project.

Part of the problem, I realized, was that Gulzar wrote in free verse. That gives a fair bit of latitude to the translator in the choice of vocabulary, in framing the lines. However, *Khooni Vaisakhi* has a consistent rhyme and metre and the lessons gleaned from the translations by Pavan didn't quite apply in my case. I discussed my dilemma with friends whose understanding of poetry is a lot better than mine. Several suggested that since *Khooni Vaisakhi* is a historical work, it is more important to accurately convey its content than to obsess over the rhythm and rhymes. They advocated that I should exercise my own poetic licence to translate it into free verse. I was grateful for their advice, but still felt that I didn't have the liberty to make such a radical departure from the original. Somewhere in the deeper recesses of the mind was Robert Frost's intemperate remark that poetry in free verse is a bit like playing tennis without a net. Implicit in his observation is the recognition that rhyme and rhythm impose constraints and the greater challenge lies in translating within the parameters set by the constraints.

It was around that time I remembered Michael Pelletier, an outstanding American diplomat who is fluent in several languages. Both of us spoke some Arabic and French and he had once given me a copy of Douglas Hofstadter's masterly *Le Ton beau de Marot – In Praise of the Music of Language*. I spent the next few days ploughing through the book, often pausing to marvel at the fecundity of Hofstader's intellect. He is quite an exceptional person – a cognitive scientist, a Pulitzer Prize winning author, a musician and a polyglot with a particular fascination with the way we work with languages. In *Le Ton beau*, he takes 'A une damoyselle malade', a short poem by sixteenth-century French poet Clement Marot and plays around with over eighty different translated versions of the poem to drive home the flexibility that a translator can enjoy. But for the specific purpose of my inquiry, Hofstadter provided the answers in Chapter 8, which is largely devoted to Alexander Pushkin's *Eugene Onegin* – a novel written entirely in verse. He takes four separate translations of the book and places select excerpts in four windows, asking the reader to rank them in order of preference. In doing so, he provides a rare perspective on the craft of four accomplished writers who had independently worked on the same text, each imparting their own distinct signature to the translation. But for me, the decisive element was the fact that each of them stuck to Pushkin's rhyme and metre even as they took some liberties with other aspects of the poem.

Hofstadter uses this example to make an important argument. Constraints like rhyme and metre are an integral part of the poet's work and it would be a travesty to ignore these factors when translating verse. He argues that the linguistic pattern of writing is no less important than the content. The relationship between form and content is so close that to select one at the expense of the other would be inexcusable.

And with that, the decision was made. The translation must attempt to be faithful to the original – not just in terms of the content but also in its rhyme and cadence.

That put my own ambivalence at rest and allowed me to complete a first draft of the translation before turning towards a couple of other aspects that were important for the project. As a poem, *Khooni Vaisakhi* is barely 900 lines (around 4000 words) long – a pamphlet that served the purpose in 1920 when it could be priced at four annas (twenty-five paise) and might have been sold in large numbers had it not been confiscated. To become a contemporary book, it needed some heft, some context and a couple of additional perspectives.

The first of these comes in the essay contributed by Professor Harbhajan Singh Bhatia, a former dean of languages at the Guru Nanak Dev University in Amritsar and a respected scholar of Punjabi literature. He provides an academic's rigour by looking at Nanak Singh as one of Punjabi's best-loved writers in the twentieth century, and at his versatility as an author who not only produced some of the most famous novels of his era but also a respectable output of plays, short stories, essays and translations.

Professor Bhatia also speaks of the author's flirtation with poetry at an early age, starting with religious poems and culminating in the unbridled patriotism and vivid imagery of *Khooni Vaisakhi*. But equally important is the way Professor Bhatia places *Khooni Vaisakhi* squarely in the milieu of poetry as a popular form of protest during the early 1920s, which establishes it as an important relic of history that provides a remarkably coherent and accurate narrative of the events and captures the mood, passions and predilections of the people of Amritsar in April 1919. He cites other contemporary Punjabi poets like Dhani Ram Chatrik, Vidhata Singh Teer, Hira Singh Dard and Firoz Din Sharaf who fearlessly took up nationalist themes in their poetry. Like *Khooni Vaisakhi*, Vidhata Singh Teer's *Teer Tarang* and Firoz Din Sharaf's *Dukh de Kirne* were also banned and confiscated by the Raj. The poignant reference to Sharaf reciting his poems at a political gathering in Jallianwala Bagh in 1923 – some four years after the massacre – provides a unique insight into those turbulent times.

The second perspective came from an unusual source and I can only thank the power of the Internet for this. I had been doing some research on the events that preceded the Jallianwala Bagh massacre and while our history books had taught us about the Rowlatt Act, the fact was that I didn't know very much about the author of that infamous legislation. In reading up about Sir Sidney Rowlatt, I stumbled upon the name of his great-grandson Justin Rowlatt. Google also revealed that until fairly recently, Justin had served as the BBC's South Asia correspondent in Delhi. I got in touch, explained my project and asked if he would contribute his unique perspective for this book. He readily agreed and I waited with bated breath, not sure about what I would get. Would it be defensive, or adversarial, or even a post facto rationalization of the kind attempted by Nick Lloyd in his *The Amritsar Massacre*? Any such worries were instantly put to rest when I received the first draft from Justin. I was struck by the empathy with which he narrated his own visit to Jallianwala Bagh, his incredibly moving conversation with the Bagh's trustee S.K. Mukherji and his dispassionate references to Sir Sidney. From a historical standpoint, Justin's excerpts from letters that Sir Sidney wrote from India to his wife are fascinating. In one of them, written after observing the grand scale on which New Delhi was being built as the imperial capital, Sir Sydney suggests that he was aware that the Empire was tottering. And yet, as Justin points out, he proceeded to draft a bill that was oblivious to both the sacrifices made by Indian troops to save the Empire during the First World War and the legitimate aspirations of educated Indians to secure a degree of self-rule. Some historians regard the Rowlatt Act and the Jallianwala Bagh massacre as the beginning of the end of the Empire, a point that is also driven home by Mahatma Gandhi's grandson Tushar Gandhi. In a conversation with Justin, he says, 'I appreciate your great-grandfather's role to provide the first nail in the coffin of the Empire.'

A third element, I thought, must be provided by us as a family. Our reminiscences about growing up near Jallianwala

Bagh; providing a personal introduction to my grandfather, known to us as our Bauji and to the world around us as Nanak Singh the Novelist; and the remarkable story of *Khooni Vaisakhi* itself, a book that was lost for nearly six decades before we found it again. I also realized that many of us don't really know a whole lot about Jallianwala Bagh, even those of us living in Amritsar. I've tried to provide a concise history of the events that led to the massacre, and of the disastrous impact of the martial law that was imposed in Punjab after the massacre. Since the Governor of Punjab Michael O'Dwyer and Brig. Gen. Reginald Dyer figure prominently in *Khooni Vaisakhi*, I've given some extra attention to both characters.

Working on this book has also helped me develop a better appreciation of the early genius of Nanak Singh as a public intellectual. Here was a person who grew up in an impoverished village and who had very little formal education. And yet, he had published his first set of poems at the age of twelve and a runaway bestseller called *Satguru Mahima* when he was twenty. In *Khooni Vaisakhi*, he starts with an invocation to the tenth Sikh Guru, Gobind Singh, refers to Lord Krishna playing Holi at Vrindavan and speaks with easy familiarity about the sacrifices of medieval Sufi mystics Shams Tabrizi and Mansour Al Haq. His vivid descriptions of Ram Navmi celebrations in Amritsar are a passionate ode to the spirit of unity between the city's Hindu, Sikh and Muslim communities. As a twenty-two-year-old shuttling between Peshawar and Amritsar, what was he reading? Where did he get these perspectives? I reread his autobiography *Meri Duniya* (My World) but failed to get any real answers.

I also read about the draconian provisions of the Rowlatt Act and of the brutal punishments administered to so many in the wake of martial law in Punjab. It renewed my respect for the raw courage that Nanak Singh – and some of the other writers of the era – demonstrated in expressing their fearless criticism of British rule. *Khooni Vaisakhi* is unsparing in its condemnation of the Raj, even accusing Brig. Gen. Dyer by name and saying that he will be remembered as a murderer for eternity.

As we get ready to commemorate the centenary of Jallianwala Bagh, I do believe that *Khooni Vaisakhi* is an apt reminder of the contribution and sacrifices of the many unsung heroes of India's freedom struggle.

Navdeep Suri
Abu Dhabi
December 2018

੧ ੳ ਵਾਹਿਗੁਰੂ ਜੀ ਕੀ ਫਤੇ ॥

ਦਿਲੀ ਮਾਰ ਪਈ ਕੁਰਲਾਣੇ ਤੈਂ ਕੀ ਦਰਦ ਨ ਆਇਆ ॥

ਖ਼ੂਨੀ ਵਿਸਾਖੀ

੧੩ ਅਪ੍ਰੈਲ ੧੯੧੯ ਨੂੰ ਅੰਮ੍ਰਿਤਸਰ

ਜਲ੍ਹਿਆਂ ਵਾਲੇ ਬਾਗ ਵਿੱਚ

ਜਨਰਲ

ਡਾਇਰ ਦੇ ਫਾਇਰ

—: ਕ੍ਰਿਤ :—

ਭਾਈ ਨਾਨਕ ਸਿੰਘ ਕਰਤਾ 'ਸਤਿਗੁਰ ਮੈਹਮਾ'

ਬਜਾਰ ਮਾਈ ਸੇਵਾਂ ਅਮ੍ਰਿਤਸਰ

੩੦ ਮਈ ਸੰਨ ੧੯੨੦

ਪ੍ਰਕਾਸ਼ਕ

ਭਾਈ ਨਾਨਕ ਸਿੰਘ ਕ੍ਰਿਪਾਲ ਸਿੰਘ ਪੁਸਤਕਾਂ

ਵਾਲੇ ਬਜਾਰ ਮਾਈ ਸੇਵਾਂ ਅੰਮ੍ਰਿਤਸਰ

ਪੰਥ ਸੇਵਕ ਪ੍ਰੈਸ ਬਜਾਰ ਮਾਈ ਸੇਵਾਂ ਅੰਮ੍ਰਿਤਸਰ ਮਾਸਟਰ
ਚੰਦਾ ਸਿੰਘ ਜੀ ਐਡੀਟਰ ਪੰਥ ਸੇਵਕ ਦੇ ਪਰਬੰਧ ਹੇਠਾਂ ਛਪਿਆ

प्रार्थना

कलगी वाळड़े शैहनशाह पिता मेरे।
चरणा तेरियां ते नमसकार सतिगुर।
तूं हैं पुशत पनाह निमाणियां दा।
दीन बंध तूं विच संसार सतिगुर।
बेड़ी पाप दे नाल भरभूर हो के,
पई ड़ोलदी है मंझधार सतिगुर।
करके मेहर इस डुबदी जांवदी नूं,
धक्का मार के लावणा पार सतिगुर।
भर के प्रेम दा इक चा देह पियाला,
जिस दे पींदियां चड़े खुमार सतिगुर।
चले नाल सरूर मसरूर हो के,
कलम दास दी तेज़ रफ़तार सतिगुर।
दसे हाल अज उहनां बेदोशियां दा,
जेहड़े देश पर होए निसार सतिगुर।
ज़ख़मां मिलदियां जांदियां सारियां नूं,
लूण छिड़क के देवे उभार सतिगुर।
फ़ोटो खिच के विछड़े सजणां दा,
रख दियां मैं विच संसार सतिगुर।
याद फेर करा दियां हिंद ताईं,
मतां देण ना दिलो विसार सतिगुर।
दासतान शहीदां दी लिखणे नूं,
दास आपदा होईया तियार सतिगुर।
तोड़ चाड़ना आपनी मेहर करके,
नानक सिंह एह करे पुकार सतिगुर।

PRAYER TO GURU GOBIND SINGH

O Father mine with the turban plumed
I bow at thy feet, my Divine Guru.
Messiah of the meek,
Saviour of the poor, my Divine Guru.
Burdened with sin, this boat of ours,
Is listing midstream, my Divine Guru.
Save it from going down in waters rough,
Guide it ashore, my Divine Guru.
Grant me thy cup of Love and Blessings,
And uplift my spirits, my Divine Guru.
Let my pen fly across the pages,
To tell this tale, my Divine Guru.
Of innocent souls laying down their lives,
For our nation's sake, my Divine Guru.
And those with wounds still bleeding and raw
Were showered with salt, my Divine Guru.
To pen a portrait of those departed ones,
Grant me the strength, my Divine Guru.
To remind my people across India,
Lest we forget their sacrifice, my Divine Guru.
To write the saga of our heroes such
Your disciple is ready, my Divine Guru.
Do help me complete this mission of mine,
Nanak Singh beseeches, O my Divine Guru.

रोलट बिल दा रौला

रोलट बिल ने घतिया आन रौला,
सारे हिंद दे लोक उदास होए।
वांग भठ दे तपिया देश सारा,
मानो सब दे लबां 'ते सास होए।
लगा मिलण अनाम अज हिंदीयां नूं,
जेहड़े मुदतां तों सीगे दास होए।
फ़ासी जमां दी गल पै गई यारो,
जिस नूं देख के बहुत निराश होए।

ROWLATT ACT CONTROVERSY

Rowlatt Act stirs up a hornet's nest
Gloom spreads like fire across the land.
A smouldering cauldron, this Hindustan,
With bated breath, trying to understand.
A reward they thought they'd get for sure
For service long, abiding each command.
Instead, as they hear of these shackles new,
Hopes are dashed, crushed into sand.

हिंद वलों पुकार

सारे हिंद ने किहा इक जान हो के,
रोलट बिल ना मूल मनज़ूर करना।
असां वारिया सब कुझ तुसां उतों,
पिआर ना दिल थीं दूर करना।
लखां सूरमे जंग कुहा दिते,
हाए कुझ तां ख़िआल हज़ूर करना।
साडे काबले रैहम इस हाल उत्ते,
रब दे वासते तरस ज़रूर करना।
मोयां होयां ताईं काहनूं मारदे हो,
हाए ऐतना नहीं ग़रूर करना।
ठोकर मार के साड़ियां दिलां ताईं,
शीशे वांग ना चकनाचूर करना।
तपे दिलां विच दुख़ा दा घत बालन,
सचमुच ना वांग तंदूर करना।
सानूं आस हैसी कुझ मिलणे दी,
तुसीं ख़ड़ा ना होर फ़तूर करना।
असीं चोर ना ठग ना ऐब कोई,
बधे होयां ने कीह कसूर करना।
नानक सिंह एस दुख़ां दे भठ अंदर,
सानूं घत ना वांग मनूर करना।

A CALL FROM INDIA

Across India echoed a clarion call
No Rowlatt we will take from you.
We gave up all we had for you
Don't spurn our sentiments for you.
O Rulers! Our sacrifices don't forget
Just bear in mind, thousands died for you.
See our plight, for Heaven's sake
Have mercy on us, compassion too.
Why hurt someone who's dying already?
Check your pride or you shall rue.
Don't scatter around more shards of glass
Of spirits crushed by you.
Don't add fuel to our sorrows any more
Don't fan the flames of fire anew.
We hoped to get a reward or two
Don't paint our fate a dark hue.
We have no vice, don't steal, don't cheat;
Bound in chains, what threat do you view?
Says Nanak Singh, Don't push us like twigs
Into furnace brimming with grief undue.

बिल पास

साडी रोदियां वासते पांदियां दी,
हाए! सुणी ना किसे फ़रिआद लोको।
धक्के धक्की चा बिल नूं पास कीता,
साडे कीरने किस नूं याद लोको।
असीं रहे हज़ूर हज़ूर करदे,
हां हज़ूर पर बडे उसताद लोको।
हाए! बंन के नवें कानून अंदर,
पीड़ सुटिया वांग कमाद लोको।

BILL PASSED

Our cries, our pleas, our calls for compassion
On deaf ears fell, all in vain.
With a push and heave, the Bill was passed
Our deeds and hopes went down the drain.
Yes Sir, Please Sir, we implored the masters
But the masters knew, holding on to the rein.
Ah! Shackled listless by a law so new
Bound tight and crushed like a bale of cane.

जलसे अते मारशल ला

आख़िरकार हुण सब निराश हो के,
लिखे आपने नूं बहि के रोण लग पए।
सचमुच हो गिया यकीन सब नूं,
भारत वरश दे भाग हुण सौण लग पए।
सारे सुख आराम काफूर होए,
केवल दुख ही दुख नज़र औण लग पए।
कोई पुछदा आण के हाल नाहीं,
सबो कूंज़ वांग करलाउण लग पए।
कम कार चा सब ने बंद कीते,
लोक वांग दीवानियां भौण लग पए।
हर इक शहिर दे विच हड़ताल होई,
सब दे कालजे मूंह नूं औण लग पए।
भारत माता दे पुत्तर इकत्तर हो के,
घत जफ़ीआं नीर वहौण लग पए।
दुख दिलां दे खोल सुणान खातर,
थाउं थाईं इजलास तद होण लग पए।
दूजी तरफ़ दे यार प्रसन्न हो के,
घरीं बैठ के ख़ुशीं मनौण लग पए।
मिशन आपने विच कामयाब हो के,
वाजे ख़ुशी दे ख़ूब वजौण लग पए।
झोली-चुक ते कौम-फ़रोश जेहड़े,
उहनां पास जा चुग़लीयां लौण लग पए।
बाग़ी चोर बदमाश बेवफ़ा कहि के,
दिल उहनां दे ख़ूब भड़कौण लग पए।
बेगुनाह ताईं गुनाहगार दस के,
वेखो मुलक दा नास करौण लग पए।

10

PROTESTS AND MARTIAL LAW

Dispirited and despondent by the turn of events
They lamented, aghast at miserable fate.
With sinking hearts, they then witnessed
A shadow spread across a nation great.
All comforts and pleasures now sadly gone
Leaving gloom and grief to stalk the state.
So sad they sound, like the wailing crane
To smile or greet they hesitate.
Shops closed and workplaces empty
Forlorn and lost, in streets they wait.
Strikes called in every city and town
Sobs muffled, they roam in a sorry state.
Those valiant sons of Bharat Mata
Shedding tears, dismayed and desolate.
Each tragedy retold, notes get compared,
Every nook and corner, a place to debate.
But a scene so different on the other side
Friends gather at homes to celebrate.
A mission accomplished, the Act is done
'Tis time for wine and feast ornate.
Their quislings, turncoats and traitors all
Come laden with gossip and tales narrate.
'Rebel', 'robber', 'scoundrel' and more
Names used against us, to aggravate.
Frame our heroes with guilt and treason
Damage they wreak on our nation great!

हाकम लोक भी उहनां दे लग आखे,
बलदी अग 'ते तेल पलटौण लग पए।
सर माईकल उडवाईर साहिब,
मारशल ला दा हुकम चड़ौन लग पए।
पकड़ पकड़ बेदोशियां आजज़ां नूं,
जेल खानियां विच पहुंचौण लग पए।
हाए! लिखदियां डिगदी कलम हथों,
रोम रोम सुण के खड़े होण लग पए।
छोटी उमर दे आजज़ां बचिआं नूं,
फड़ के मछीयां वांग तड़फौण लग पए।
नाल टिकटिकी बंन निमाणियां नूं,
बैंत मार के खल लहौण लग पए।
मास तूंबियां नाल उडौण लग पए।
लहू नाल इशनान करौण लग पए।
मावां बाप उहनां दे जे कोल आवण,
धक्के मार के पिछांह हटौण लग पए।
अठ वजे तों बाद जो बाहर निकले,
गोली मारन दा हुकम सुनौण लग पए।
मातम नज़र आवे चारों तरफ़ उदों,
सबे दुखां दे सोहले गौण लग पए।
नानक सिंघ की खोल के हाल दसे,
जेहड़े दुख पंजाब ते औण लग पए।

And a smirk of delight it brings upon the rulers
Who divide and rule, planting seeds of hate!
Sir Michael O'Dwyer, armed with a pen
Brings martial law and a Police State.
Young men of ours, innocent, upright
Sent packing to jail at an alarming rate.
My pen shudders, drops from trembling hands
Ah! Tales of torture – so deliberate.
Young boys flogged and bleeding lie
Like fish out of water, in dire straits.
Tied to poles and whipped with canes
Skin peels, their tender backs lacerate.
Flesh and bone do take the brunt
As streams of blood rush to the gate.
In desperate search their parents reach
Pushed rudely, ordered: Go home and wait!
Stay in your homes, don't dare come out!
Or face a bullet, if it's later than eight!
A funereal spirit pervades the air,
A stifled wail, a silent dirge and a pain innate.
Says Nanak Singh, Ah! The pain of Punjab!
Words choke as I speak, they suffocate.

अमृतसर दे सिर बीती

होर शहिरा दे विच जो रंग वरते,
एस शहिर दे वी उहो रंग होए।
रोलट बिल दे पास दी ख़बर सुण के,
दिल सारियां दे डाढ़े तंग होए।
यारो एह अनहोणी गल सुण के,
शहर वासीयां दे ज़रद रंग होए।
नानक सिंह तूं खोल के दस छेती,
जेहड़े अगांह नूं नवें परसंग होए।

THE FATE OF AMRITSAR

Scenes like these from village and town
Played out too in our city sublime
Rowlatt's passage that fateful day
Numbed every heart, 'twas a crime.
A law so foul it seemed unreal
Faces ashen, shocked by new paradigm.
Says Nanak Singh, Let's move on apace
Of events unfolding, one at a time.

राम नोमी दी धूम – धाम
अते हिंदू मुसलमानां दे पिआर दा सबूत

सारे सिख हिंदू अते मुसलमानां,
रल मिल एह पुरब मनाईया सी।
मुसलमानां ने अज ईतफ़ाक वाला,
एह अदुती सबूत विखाईया सी।
भावें पुरब सी असल विच हिंदूआं दा,
अैपर मोमनां ख़ूब सजाईया सी।
उस दिन दी की मैं गल दसां,
अजब समां करतार लिआईया सी।
'डाकटर किचलू ते सत्या पाल साहिब',
जिन्हां अज दा वक्त दिखाईया जी।
गले दोहां दे फुलां दे हार पा के,
सारे शहिर नूं दरशन कराईया जी।
हर एक हिंदू मुसलमान ताईं,
दिलों जाणदा माई दा जाईया जी।
कदी ऐदां दा प्रेम ना किसे डिठा,
जगत जदों दा रब बणाईया जी।
एह तां नवां ही प्रेम दा बीज ऐथे,
किसे अरश तों आण के लाईया जी।
दूरी सब दे दिलां तों दूर होई,
वीर वीर ताईं नज़र आईया जी।
पाणी इक गलास दे विच पीता,
ख़ाणा इक थां सब ने खाईया जी।

RAM NAVAMI CELEBRATIONS AMID HINDU–MUSLIM UNITY

Hindus and Muslims they gathered together
To rejoice at a festival, O my friends.
Brotherhood conveyed by Muslims that day
Beyond incredible it was, my friends.
A festival of Hindus though it was
Muslims made it just their own, my friends.
'Tis hard to describe this feeling new
A miracle, it truly seemed, my friends.
Doctors Saifudin, Satyapal together
Tread on a path united, my friends.
Feted with garlands, our stalwart duo
Sent out a message clear, my friends.
Their friendship displayed a bond so strong
Hindu Muslim were the same, my friends.
Such harmony never seen before
Since God made this world, O my friends.
The seed of friendship between these faiths
Descended from heaven itself, my friends.
Discord and difference seemed to vanish
Each saw the other as brother, my friends.
Shared the same glass to drink their water,
Sat down for meals together, my friends.

सारी उमर दे विछड़े वीरनां नूं,
अज आप करतार मिलाईया जी।
उस दिन हर जगा 'ते मुसलमानां,
दुद्ध दीआं छबीलां चा खोलीयां जी।
नाल हिंदूआं सब ने होए शामल,
पाईयां फुलां दीयां भर झोलीयां जी।
कीती हिंदूआं दी दिल खोल सेवा,
थाऊ थाई बनाई के टोलीयां जी।
मानो कृष्ण ने अज प्रसन्न हो के,
ब्रिंदाबन विच खेड़ीयां होलीयां जी।
होणी आखदी सुणो नादान लोको,
हटां कास नूं अज चा खोलीयां जी।
भलके फेर है तुसां हड़ताल करनी,
नाले वसणगीयां तुसां पर गोलीयां जी।

Like brothers separated since their birth
Stood united now by a miracle, my friends.
Each Muslim tried to outdo the other
Served sweetened drinks to all, my friends.
Each one stood with their Hindu mate
Showering flowers on devotees all, my friends.
Groups joyous lined up on the festive route
Cheering the jubilant Hindu parade, my friends.
Lord Krishna seemed charmed by the sight
Like Holi played at Vrindavan, my friends.
But Fate, it had some different plans
Why open your shops today, my friends?
The town will be on strike tomorrow
You'll catch a hail of bullets, my friends.

दूसरे दिन डाकटर सतपाल ते डाकटर सैफ़ोदीन किचलू दा ग्रिफ़तार हो जाणा

सतपाल अते सैफ़ोदीन ने जी,
अजे रज दीदार ना कल दिता।
अज चाड़ के उहनां नूं मोटरां 'ते,
पता नहीं केहड़ी तरफ़ घल दिता।
बलदी अग 'ते तेल चा घतिउ ने,
दुखे दिलां नूं पकड़ के सल दिता।
कई होर भी लीडरां पिआरियां नूं,
रहिन वासते जेल महल दिता।

THE NEXT DAY: DR SAIFUDIN AND DR SATYAPAL ARRESTED

Both Saifudin and Satyapal so quickly gone
We'd been with them barely a while.
Bundled silently and taken to a place unknown
Spirited secretly in a car driven for many a mile.
Oil sprinkled again on embers fresh
Grieving hearts stung by this action vile.
Other leaders well-known and beloved too
Found prison and cells their new exile.

वाक कवी

दुखां विच इक सुख दी झलक आ के,
निकल गई जिउं जांवदी रेल यारो।
दीवा खुशी दा रता कल टहिकिआ सी,
अज डुल गिया उस 'चों तेल यारो।
ज़रा निकले सी कल कैद विचों,
अज फेर पै गए विच जेल यारो।
है सी कल आज़ादी दा दिन डिठा,
अज फेर पै गई नकेल यारो।
सुके बाग नूं दिता सी किसे पाणी,
अज फेर उह सुक गई वेल यारो।
कल होई सिपाही दी सज़ा पूरी,
अज फेर पै गई नकेल यारो।
पंछी आलणे 'चों ज़रा निकलिया सी,
अज फेर आ वजी गुलेल यारो।
नानक सिंह तकदीर नूं कौण रोके,
जेहड़ा रब वरतावणा खेल यारो।

THE POET'S THOUGHTS

That moment brief, of joy amid sorrow
Gone like a streaking train, my friends.
That lamp of joy, which shimmered awhile
Ran out of its oil too soon, my friends.
'Twas after a few days of release from prison
Thrown right back into jail, my friends.
The dawn of freedom that blinked yesterday
Got snuffed out behind the bars, my friends.
Our parched garden bloomed so briefly
Is withering much too soon, my friends.
So short, their freedom outside the jail
Alas! they're back in chains, my friends
Like a bird that barely left its nest
By slingshot is brought down, my friends.
Says Nanak Singh, You can't fight fate
God Himself is playing with you, my friends.

शहिर वासीआं दा फ़रिआद करन लई जाणा ते अगों पुल तों गोलीआं दी वरखा होणी

फड़े जाण दी ख़बर सी जदों पहुंची,
लोक बहुत होए बेकार पिआरे।
ड़ाढ़े ग़ज़ब दी बिजली पई आ के,
ढाहीं मार रोंदे ज़ारो ज़ार पिआरे।
खाण पीण ते खुशी आराम भुले,
लोकी छड़ बैठे कंम कार पिआरे।
दसां मिंटां दे विच हड़ताल हो गई,
सारे शहिर अंदर इको वार पिआरे।
चिहरे ग़मां दे नाल मुरझाण लगे,
रंग हो गिया वांग वसार पिआरे।
सारे लोक फिर होए इकत्तर जांदे,
पास हाक्मां करन पुकार पिआरे।
लोकीं निकले शहिर तों बाहर जदों,
होण लगे सन पुल तां पार पिआरे।
अगे पुल 'ते खड़े हो फ़ौजीआं ने,
रफ़लां कीतीआं बीड़ त्यार पिआरे।
ज़रा तरस ना आईया ज़ालमां नूं,
गोली छड़ दिती काड़ काड़ पिआरे।
घरों गए सन लैण इनसाफ़ यारो,
जांदे मौत दे होए शिकार पिआरे।
कुझ मोए ते कुझ कंबख़त बाकी,
मुड़े पिछांह नूं होए बेज़ार पिआरे।
नानक सिंह पर लिखे नूं कौण मेटे,
जिहड़ा लिखिआ धुरों करतार पिआरे।

THE CITIZENS' PETITION IS MET WITH
A HAIL OF BULLETS ON THE BRIDGE

The news of our leaders' arrest is heard
And a pall of despair descends, O friends.
Like bolt of lightning it strikes them deep
And thousands wail out in grief, O friends.
No food, no water, no comfort for them
Left home and hearth and work, O friends.
In the blink of an eye, the strike takes hold
Spreads across the city, O my friends.
Like wilted flowers, faces drawn and grim
Our youth looked painfully pale , O friends.
Upset, they gathered in numbers large
To argue and plead with the Rulers, O friends.
Through famous gates of their city walled,
They headed for the railway bridge, O friends.
Saw soldiers positioned across the bridge,
Guns cocked and ready to fire, O friends.
Not a shred of mercy, these tyrants showed
Bang-bang the bullets kept firing, O friends.
Had gone to seek some justice but
They died right then and there, O friends.
Some did survive that fatal day
Turned back in horror true, O friends.
Says Nanak Singh, You can't change Fate
That's writ by God Himself, O friends.

मुरदे ते ज़ख़मी

आख़र रोंवदे पिटदे मुड़े घर नूं,
सारे लोक हो के परेशान यारो।
मुरदे चुक के आपने मोढियां 'ते,
सारे शहिर दे विच पहुंचाण यारो।
रातीं हाल बाज़ार मसीत अंदर,
सारे मुरदियां ताईं टिकाण यारो।
सुबाह चुक के तरफ़ सुलतानविंड़ दी,
कबरसतान दे विच पहुंचाण यारो।
लखां आदमी नाल जनाज़ियां दे,
तुरे जांवदे होए हैरान यारो।
सारे हिंदूआं सिखां ते मोमनां नूं,
ड़ाढा लगा एह ग़ज़ब दा बान यारो।
इको जिसम इको दरद इको,
सारे मज़हब होए एको जान यारो।
इक होर असचरज़ दी गल देखी,
जेहड़ी करदी है बहुत हैरान यारो।
हिंदू सिख उदों या–हुसैन कहिंदे,
मुसलमान कहिंदे राम राम यारो।
अख़ीर जाऐ पहुंचे कबरसतान अंदर,
सारे सिख हिंदू मुसलमान यारो।
इक जगा 'ते फूकिआ हिंदूआं नूं,
दूजी जमा मोमन दफ़नान यारो।
बाकी ज़ख़मीआं सहिकदे लुछदियां नूं,
पास डाकटर तुरंत पहुंचण यारो।
नानक सिंह अगांह नूं किवें होई,
सुणो अगली भी दासतान यारो।

THE DEAD AND WOUNDED

They straggled, drenched in anger and tears,
Distraught they truly were, my friends.
Carried corpses on their shoulders bent
Limped back to their city sad, my friends.
Hall Bazaar's mosque was the night's abode
For dead bodies placed in rows, my friends.
Heaved up next morning and off once again
To Sultanwind's graveyard large, my friends.
Funeral processions joined by thousands more
Walked angrily, dazed and distraught, my friends.
Hindu, Sikh and Muslim strode side by side
Hearts pierced by arrows sharp, my friends.
The same grief and pain they shared
Each bound by sorrow same, my friends.
Then a sight most wondrous was seen
It left us amazed and awed, my friends.
'Ya Hussain!' cried out the Hindus and Sikhs
As Muslims echoed 'Ram Ram!', my friends.
And thus they reached the graveyard together
Hindu, Muslim and also the Sikh, my friends.
Funeral pyres flamed for Hindus and Sikhs
With Muslims buried alongside, my friends.
Others injured, wounded and limping slow
Were taken to doctors from there, my friends.
Asks Nanak Singh, what happened next?
Stay on and listen with me, my friends.

कई होर लीडर फड़े जाण 'ते
खटीकां दी ढ़ाब पर जलसा होणा

बारां तरीक अप्रैल नूं ख़बर मिली,
जिस नूं सुण के होए दिलगीर सबे।
कई होर लीडर फड़े जावने दी,
ख़बर गई कलेजड़े चीर सबे।
कट्टे होए खटीकां दी ढ़ाब उत्ते,
चले रल के घत वहीर सबे।
बेगुनाहां दे दुखां नूं याद कर के,
छमा छम वहांवदे नीर सबे।
सारे मिल के करन सलाह लगे,
कंहदे सोचीए कोई तदबीर सबे।
करीई अरज़ीआं भेज फ़रिआद अपणी,
मारे जांवदे बिनां तकसीर सबे।
भलके फेर चा करो इक होर जलसा,
कट्टे होए गरीब अमीर सबे।
विच जलियाँ बाग इक्ट्ठ होसी,
भलके आवणा उस थां वीर सबे।
पंज वजे कल शाम दे ठीक उथे,
पहुंच जावणा वक्त अख़ीर सबे।
नानक सिंह ना परत के किसे औणा,
रखो दिलां विच अपने धीर सबे।

A RALLY AT DHAB KHATIKAN
AS MORE LEADERS ARRESTED

Dawned April the twelfth with still more news
That grieved the hearts of one and all.
Of leaders picked up and put in jails
Leaving followers wondering, one and all.
To Dhab Khatikan their feet took them
'What next?' they worried, one and all.
No wrong was done by these innocent souls
Cried friends of theirs, one and all.
Some better way must surely be there,
They fretted and fumed, one and all.
Should we make one final appeal?
Beg for mercy, wondered one and all.
Let's meet tomorrow one more time
Gather rich and poor, one and all.
Let Jallianwala Bagh be that place
Go spread the word, to one and all.
At five o'clock we must be there
Make sure you convey this to one and all.
Says Nanak Singh, Only be prepared
For your final journey, one and all.

वाक कवी

हाए! ग़ज़ब! कंबख़त बेदोशियां नूं,
कूचे कातल लै चली तकदीर खिच के।
होणी आखदी जावसो नस किथे,
पैरीं मौत ने पाए ज़ंजीर खिच के।
छेती जाईके सीस निवाए रखों,
डाईर आवसी हुणे शमशीर खिच के।
उथे आबोहयात दा खूह भरिआ,
हथीं आपनी पीवणा नीर खिच के।
होई किस तरां नाल कतलाम उथे,
नानक सिंह तूं दस तसवीर खिच के।

THE POET'S THOUGHTS

Oh God! These innocent men taken
To killing fields, by Providence.
No place to hide, nowhere to run
Feet shackled by lurking Death intense
Crouch low, keep your heads near the ground!
For Dyer's coming, and there's no defense.
Your body and chest will seem to him,
A target tempting as bullets commence.
The well that often meets your thirst
May quench its own with bodies of men.
Says Nanak Singh, Must paint the picture
Of the massacre brutal, with my pen.

जलियां वाले बाग़ विच इक्ट्ठ

पंच वजे अप्रैल दी तेहरवीं नूं,
लोकीं बाग़ वल होए रवान चले।
दिलां विच इनसाफ़ दी आस रख के,
सारे सिख हिन्दू मुसलमान चले।
विरले आदमी शहिर विच रहे बाकी,
सब बाल ते बिरध जवान चले।
अज दिलां दे दुख सुणान चले,
सगों आपने गले कटवाण चले।
छड़ दिउ हुण आसरा जीवने दा,
क्योंकि तुसीं हुण छड जहान चले।
किस ने आवणा परत के घरां अंदर,
दिल दा दिलां विच छोड़ अरमान चले।
जलिआं वालड़े उजड़े बाग़ ताई,
ख़ून डोल के सबज़ बणान चले।
अज होएके सब पतंग कट्ठे,
उपर शमा सरीर जलाण चले।
हां हां जीवने तों ड़ाढ़े तंग आ के,
रुठी मौत नूं आप मनाण चले।
अनल–हक मनसूर दे वांग यारो,
सूली आपनी आप गड़ाण चले।
वांग शमस तबरेज़ दे खुशी हो के,
खलां पुठीआं अज लुहाण चले।

THE GATHERING IN JALLIANWALA BAGH

As the clock struck five on thirteenth April
They all gather in the Bagh, my friends.
Seeking justice fair and honour, they stand
Sikhs, Hindus, Muslims together, my friends.
Folks young and old, and lads went too
For only a handful had stayed back, my friends.
They went to speak, to share their grief
Place lives at stake without fear, my friends.
Worrying no more about their precious lives
They left this world behind, my friends.
With slender hope of coming back home
Desires and dreams abandoned too, my friends.
With their own blood, they wanted to bloom
The parched soil of the Bagh, my friends.
Like swarms of moths, they gathered around
To be singed by violent flames, my friends.
Fed up with life, they courted death
Forcing Yama to accept their will, my friends.
Like Mansour, who said, 'I am the Truth!'
When he knew he'd meet the gallows, my friends.
Like Shams Tabrizi, whose quest for God
Ended up in a painful death, my friends.

पंछी बना दे होएके सब कट्ठे,
भुखे बाज़ नूं अज रजाण चले।
ज़ालम डाईर दी तिर्खा मिटावणे नूं,
अज खून दी नदी वहाण चले।
अज शहर विच पैणगे वैण डूंघे,
वसदे घरां नूं थेह बणाण चले।
सीस आपने रख के तली उत्ते,
भारत माता दी भेंट चढ़ाण चले।
कोई मोड़ लौ रब दे बंदिआं नूं,
यारो! मौत नूं आप बुलाण नूं,
मावां लाड़ले बचिआं वालिओ नी!
लाल तुसां दे जान गवाण चले।
भैणो पिआरीओ! वीर ना जाण देणे,
विछड़ तुसां तों अज नादान चले।
पती रोक लौ पिआरोओं नारीओ नी!
अज तुसां नूं करन वैराण चले।
पिआरे बचिओं! जफीआं घत मिल लौ,
पिता तुसां नूं अज रुलाण चले।
जा के रोक लौ, जाण ना मूल देणे,
मतां उके ही तुसां तों जाण चले।
नानक सिंह पर उन्हां नूं कौण रोके,
जिहड़े मुलक पर होण कुरबान चले।

Like birds from the woods, they flocked together
So the hawk could have his fill, my friends.
To quench Dyer's deadly thirst
With streams of blood their own, my friends.
Ah! My city mourns with grief today
Happy homes lie shattered because they go.
Heads held high offered for sacrifice
For Bharat Mata's pride and honour, they go.
Pray, stop these valiant souls of God!
Straight to the abyss, they rise and go.
O mothers, watch your precious sons
To give up their youthful lives, they go.
O sisters, hold back your brothers dear
You won't see them again once they go.
O wives, hang on to your dear beloveds
Or you'll spend your lives widowed, if they go.
O children, go run and hug your fathers
'Cause you'll be orphans if they go.
Stop them, hold them, do what you can
They won't come back, once they go.
Says Nanak Singh, Can't stop them now
For nation's sake to die they go.

जनरल डाईर ने आउणा ते गोली चलणी

ठीक वक्त साढ़े पंज वजे दा सी,
लोक जमां होए कई हज़ार पिआरे,
लीडर देश दा दुख फरोलणे नूं,
लैक्चर देंवदे सन वारो वार पिआरे।
कहदे जीवणा असां दा होएआं औखा,
किथे जाइके करीऐ पुकार पिआरे।
कोई सुझदी नहीं तदबीर सानूं,
ड़ाढ़े होए हां असीं लाचार पिआरे।
अजे लफ़ज़ तदबीर मूंह विच हैसी,
उधर फ़ौज ने धूड़ धुमा दिती।
थोड़ी देर पिछे फ़ौज गोरखे दी,
जनरल डाइर ने अगांह वधा दिती।
दे के हुक्म नहक निमाणिआं 'ते,
काड़ काड़ बंधूक चला दिती।
मिटां विच ही कई हज़ार गोली,
उहनां ज़ालमां ख़तम करा दिती।
गोली की एह गड़ा सी कहर वाला,
वांग छोलिआं भुने जवान उथे।
कई छातीआं छानणी वांग होईआं,
अैसे ज़ुलमां मारे निशन उथे।
इक पलक दे विच कुरलाट मचिआ,
धूंआं धार हो गिया असमान उथे।
कई सूरमे पाणी ना मंग सके,
रही कईआं दी तड़पदी जान उथे।

BRIG. GEN. DYER ARRIVES,
GUNFIRE BEGINS

Five-thirty sharp the clock had struck
Thousands gathered in the Bagh, my friends.
Leaders came to lament the nation's woes
Taking turns to speak out loud, my friends.
Voiced grievance, hardship, anger, sorrow
Saying, no one listens to us, my friends.
What can we do, what options left?
Can't see any ray of light, my friends.
Those words forlorn, they barely voiced
Came soldiers thundering down, my friends.
At Dyer's command, those Gurkha troops
Gathered in a formation tight, my friends.
Under the tyrant's orders, they opened fire
Straight into innocent hearts, my friends.
And fire and fire and fire they did
Some thousands of bullets were shot, my friends.
Like searing hail they felled our youth
A tempest not seen before, my friends.
Riddled chests and bodies slid to the ground
Each one a target large, my friends.
Haunting cries for help did rend the sky
Smoke rose from smouldering guns, my friends.
Just a sip of water was all they sought
Valiant youth lay dying in the dust, my friends.

भीड़े राह हैसन इस बाग़ दे जी,
एह रोकिया उहनां ने आण उथे।
कोई राह ना जाण नूं रिहा बाकी,
किदां बच करके निकल जाण उथे।
कोई बचिया होउ नसीब वाला,
नहीं तां सारिआं ने दिते प्रान उथे।
कई गोलीआं खाईके नठ भजे,
रसते विच ही डिग मर जाण उथे।
कईआं नसदिआं नूं गोली काड़ वजी,
झट पट ही दिते प्राण उथे।
पल विच ही लोथा दे ढेर लग गए,
कोई सके ना मूल पछाण उथे।
गिणती सिखां दी बहुत ही नज़र आवे,
भावें बहुत हिंदू मुसलमान उथे।
सोहणे सूरमे छैल छबीलडे जी,
हाए तड़फ़दे शेर जवान उथे।
सोहणे केस खुले मिट्टी विच रुलण,
सुते लंमीआं चादरां ताण उथे।
नानक सिंह ना पुछदा बात कोई,
राखा उहनां दा इक भगवान उथे।

That narrow lane to enter the Bagh
Sealed off on Dyer's command, my friends.
No exit, no escape, no way out was left
Making the Bagh a deathly trap, my friends.
A fortunate few somehow survived
While most died then and there, my friends.
Some ran with bullets ripping their chest
Stumbling to their painful end, my friends.
Others caught the bullet while running away
Dropping lifeless in awkward heaps, my friends.
In minutes, the Bagh so strewn with corpses
None knew just who was who, my friends.
Many of them did look like Sikhs
Amid Hindus and Muslims plenty, my friends.
In the prime of their youth, our bravehearts lay
Gasping for one last breath, my friends.
Long hair lay matted in blood and grime
In slumber deep they sleep, my friends.
Says Nanak Singh, Who knows their state
But God the One and Only, my friends.

लोकां ने आपने संबंधियां दीआं लाशां लै औणिआं ते विरलाप करने

रोंदे पिटदे लोक संबंधियां नूं।
ढूंढण वासते मुरदियां वल जांदे।
मापे वेख के आपने बचिआं नूं, हाए!
वांग पतंगे दे जल जांदे।
मोए लाड़ले जिन्हां दे पुत्त यारो,
सीने नाल कटारीआं सल जांदे।
पथर वांग जिन्हां दड़े दिल पथर,
नीर उन्हां दी अंखीउं चल जांदे।

PEOPLE WAILING AS THEY BRING THE CORPSES OF LOVED ONES

With faces drawn and muffled sobs
They sift through the corpses in silent fear.
Like moth on a flame, hearts burn to ashes
On seeing the fate of sons so dear.
Ah! The pain of losing a child so precious
Like the heart is pierced with dagger or spear.
Grief inconsolable melts the toughest of souls
Even faces most stoic shed tear after tear.

मापिआं दा आपणे मुरदा बच्चिआं नूं देख के विरलाप करना

मुरदा बच्चिआं नूं सीने नाल ला के,
कहदे हाए एह जुलम अज होवणा सी।
मेरे लाल मैं वारी आं जाग छेती,
जंगल विच आ के काहनूं सौंवणा सी।
बिनां पुछिआं लंबड़े राह पिउं,
सानूं दस के विदिआ होवणा सी।
रता असां दा साथ उड़ीक लैंदों,
घड़ी दो घड़ी चाई खलोवणा सी।
जेकर आ गिया सी तेरा काल बच्चा,
माई बाप नूं अगे चा ढोवणा सी।
नानक सिंह पर लिखे नूं कौण मेटे,
एह हुक्म करतार दा होवणा सी।

PARENTS MOURN THEIR DEPARTED CHILDREN

Clutching lifeless bodies of precious sons
Parents mourn the abject horrors of the day.
My child, oh! Wake up just once more
What makes you sleep in a place so grey?
You left us alone for a voyage so long
No goodbye you bid, nor farewell did you say.
Couldn't you wait for a while longer
To let us join you, on your eternal way?
If Time indeed had come to part
Your parents could join, without delay.
Says Nanak Singh, You can't fight Fate
When the Master orders, you just obey.

नारीआं दा आपने पतिआं नूं देख के रोणा

नारां रोंदीआं पति दे पास बहि के,
कहिण पति! अज कहिर दी रात होई।
ज़ालम रावण ने राम जी जुदा कीते,
सीता रोंवदी नूं प्रभात होई।
हंझू डिगदे छमा छम अखीआं तों,
रंगत अंखां दी लाल बनात होई।
शाम पिआरिआ! बंसरी सुट बैठों,
हाए अज केही चुप चाप होई।
गोले गड़े दे पए गए फ़सल उते,
केही जुलम दी अज बरसात होई।
धरम राज दे पासे मैं करां अरज़ी,
केही नाल मेरे वारदात होई।
काग़ज़ दिल ते हड़ां दी कलम घड़ के,
खून सियाही 'ते जिगर दवात होई।
नानक सिंह ना रज के मुख ड़िठा,
अजे रज के ना गलबात होई।

WIVES MOURN THEIR HUSBANDS

Wives sat beside their husbands, wailing,
Oh God! What calamity this night did spawn.
Evil Ravana snatched away my Rama
Leaving Sita grieving until the break of dawn.
As tears streak down in ceaseless flow
Her eyes bloodshot and face so drawn.
A pall of silence now haunts each home
O Lord Krishna! Your flute is gone.
Untimely hailstorm has wrecked my crop
Bringing rain of misery in its terrible wake.
O Dharamraj, I must ask of you
What have you done, for Goodness's sake?
Ah! My heart the paper, my blood the ink.
To create this pen, my bones did break.
Says Nanak Singh, She was much too young
Lonely and bereft, her heart does ache.

भैणां दा विरलाप

भैणां कहिंदीयां वीर वे! छड़ तुरिउं,
वरज रही पर नस के आईउं वे।
हाए, रब दे वासते पाए रहीआं,
हथीं पै के बाग नूं धाईउं वे।
खारे चाड़िआं काल ने अज तैनूं,
जंज जमां दी नाल लै आईउं वे।
नानक सिंह जा के उस शहिर वासिउं,
जिथों परत के फेर ना आइउं वे।

THE LAMENT OF SISTERS

O brother of mine! Why did you go?
To my prayers and pleas, you paid no heed.
'For God's sake, don't go to the Bagh today!'
You fought and left with extra speed.
Your marriage rituals hadn't yet begun
And the wedding party arrives with Yama's breed.
Says Nanak Singh, You've gone to the place
One never comes back from, the Lord decreed.

वाक कवी

की मैं दूसरे दिन दा हाल दसां,
दिल कहे एह हाल सुणा नाहीं।
मंडी मुरदिआं दी थाउं थाईं लगी,
किते दिसे वपारी दा नां नाहीं।
अज मौत ने वी मूंह तोड़ दिता,
कहिंदी बस हुण होर लै जा नाहीं।
ड़ाढ़े सुते ने चादरां ताण सारे,
कोई तकदा अज उतांह नाहीं।
हाए लाड़ले मावां दे पुत सोहणे,
धुपे पए अज रुख दी छां नाहीं।
कल खुशी दे नाल सी घरों आए,
अज दिसदे उहनां दे नां नाहीं।
डेरे विच उजाड़ दे आण लाए,
मानो जावणा कदे गिरां नाहीं।
नानक सिंह ना इन्हां विच कोई ऐसा,
जिस 'ते होई बंदूक दी ठाह नाहीं।

THE POET'S THOUGHTS

What can I say about the morrow
Don't whisper a word, my heart warns me.
At every corner, bodies strewn in rows
In the bazaar of corpses, no vendor to see.
Even Death, it seems has turned its face
'Enough!' it says, 'Just let things be.'
White sheets cover their slumber deep
None lifts his head, nor opens his eyes for me.
Those handsome lads of indulgent mothers
Now lay in scorching heat, without shade of a tree.
Happily they left homes, the previous day,
Now gone, abandoned, their names unknown.
Like hermits, who leave their homes and kin
Just gone away, into some different zone.
Says Nanak Singh, Every one of them
Got a bullet that carried his name alone.

मुरदियां दे ससकार ते दफ़न होणे

चौदां तरीक जा के शहिर वासीआं ने,
लौथां आण शहीदां दीआं कढ़ीआं जी।
भला चुकिआं कियों तक पवे पूरी,
आख़र लद के आंदीआं गडीआं जी।
थां-थां लोथां दे ढ़ेर लगाए दिते,
विचे छोटीआं ते विचे वड़ीआं जी।
अगन देवता अज निहाल होईआ,
लाटां वेख, असमान तक छड़ीआं जी।
वाहवा साहिबा! खेल अचरज तेरे,
लोक तकदे अखीआं अड़ीआं जी।
थोड़ी देर तक खाक दे ढ़ेर लग गए,
बाकी रहीआं शहीदां दीआं हड़ीआं जी।
मुसलमानां ने कड के अड मुरदे,
कबरसतान दे विच पहुंचा दिते।
अज चाड़ के जंज सब लाड़िआं दी,
मानो मौत दे नाल परना दिते।
यारो! कड के महिल चुबारियां 'चों,
विच गोर दे सब बिठा दिते।
नानक सिंह एह मोए नहीं मूल यारो,
सगों मोए भी इहनां जिवा दिते।

CREMATION AND BURIAL OF BODIES

Folks headed for the Bagh on the fourteenth
To reclaim the bodies of heroes who died.
Too many they were to carry on their backs
Carts brought in bodies laid side by side.
Corpses began to emerge from every corner
Some large and others oh so small, we cried.
Lord Agni smiled eagerly, with warm delight
Raising tongues of flames for the feast he spied.
My Lord! Your game's beyond our ken
Wide-eyed, we gazed, just mesmerized.
Some heaps of ashes, some pieces of bone,
'Tis all that's left of our bravehearts, we sighed.
The Muslims segregate their own departed
Amidst wails, a burial quiet in the graveyard near.
Snatched wantonly in their bloom of youth
In union eternal with Death, they disappear.
For those who dwelt in houses grand
A humble grave, their abode austere.
Says Nanak Singh, Don't believe they're dead
They'll go and wake the dead, you hear?

शहीदां दी आवाज़

जा के देख लौ जलिआं दे बाग़ अंदर,
की कुझ रहे शहीद पुकार लोको।
मोहणे मार के आख रहे हिंद ताईं,
तुसां दा वेखिआं पिआर लोको।
असीं तुसां दे लई शहीद होए,
सारे छड़ के बाग़ परवार लोको।
अख़ीर असीं भी आदमी तुसां वरगे,
करनी जाणदे ऐश बहार लोको।
अैपर छौड़ के घरां दे सुख सारे,
जानां दितीआं तुसां पर वार लोको।
छाती ढाह के वांगरां चांद मारी,
लईआं गोलीआं असां सहार लोको।
साडे सीनियां नूं ज़रा आण वेखो,
छेक पए ने कई हज़ार लोको।
तुसीं घरीं बैठे मौजां विसार लोको।
साडे नाल की तुसां दा वाईदा सी,
चंगा पालिआ कौल इकरार लोको।
कोठे चाड़ के पौड़ीआं खिच लईआं,
चंगे वीर तुसीं वफ़ादार लोको।
साडी पीड़ अज तुसां विसार दिती,
सानूं अगांह कर के धक्के मार लोको।
साडा करज़ है तुसां पर बहुत सारा,
जिहड़ा चुकिआ तुसीं उधार लोको।

VOICES OF MARTYRS

Make time to visit this Bagh of ours
Echoing tales of our gallant souls, O friends.
With a heavy heart, they mock our nation
Thanks so much for your love, O friends!
For this land of ours we gave our lives
Left family, home and hearth, O friends.
Ordinary folk we were, so much like you
Loved life and partied too, O friends.
Without a thought, we left it all
To serve you until we die, O friends.
Gave torsos ours for their target practise
Feted each bullet they fired, O friends.
Look closely at our bodies sieved
A thousand wounds you'll see, O friends.
You stayed at home, revelling in your life
And exiled us from your hearts, O friends.
How could you promise and forget
What a way to honour your word, O friends.
Sent us to the roof and pulled the ladder
So true and loyal you stayed, O friends.
Took us to the edge and pushed us over
Forgetting the pain we bore, O friends.
There's a hefty debt you owe to us
It must be settled soon, O friends.

सानूं विछड़ियां नूं ऐनी मुदत होई,
बणी अजे तक ना यादगार लोको।
साडे वांग ही तुसां भी त्यार रहिणा,
सबे ग़फ़लतां दिउ विसार लोको।
बणो मरद ते मुलक दी करो सेवा,
मतां भुल जावे इकरार लोको।
नानक सिंह है मौत ज़रूर आउणी,
क्यों ना देश पर होवे निसार लोको।

No plaque, no bust, no monument built
To mark the place where we died, O friends.
Be ready now to take this mantle heavy
'Tis time to discard your follies, O friends.
Be a man, be prepared to serve the nation
Dare not forget this promise, O friends.
Says Nanak Singh, One day you'll die for sure
Why not die for nation's sake, O friends.

शहीदां वलों जनरल डाईर नूं सरटीफ़िकेट

हाए हाए! डाईर उ बेतरस डाईर,
काहनूं आईउं तूं विच पंजाब डाईर।
जुलम करदिआं तैनूं ना तरस आईआ,
की तूं पीती सी उदों शराब डाईर?
लै हुण रज के पी लै लहू साडा,
असां तेरे लई भरिआ तालाब डाईर।
जिवें मारिआ इ असां बेदोशिआं नूं,
लवे तैथों वी रब हिसाब डाईर।
हाए पापीआ! ऐवें ना हक साडे,
कीते कालजे भुन कबाब डाईर।
भला दस मज़लूमां 'ते जुलम करके,
कहिडा खटिआ तुध सवाद डाईर।
जिवें साडिआ इ साडे सीनिआं नूं,
तूं भी होऐगा तिवें खराब डाईर।
मर के जावेंगा विच तूं दोज़ख़ां दे,
उथे मिलणगे बहुत आज़ाब डाईर।
फेर रब दी विच दरगाह जा के,
दस देवेंगा की जवाब डाईर।
अज ज़ालमा सारे जहान वलों,
लिआ ख़ूनी दा तूं ख़िताब डाईर।
साडा शहिनशाह तैनू इस पाप बदले,
वेखीं करेगा किवें ग़रकाब डाईर।
नानक सिंह मसूमां पर जुलम करना,
केहड़ी लिखिआ विच किताब डाईर।

THE MARTYRS' CERTIFICATE TO DYER

Shame on you, you merciless Dyer
What brought you to Punjab, O Dyer?
Not a sign of mercy unleashing such horror
How badly were you drunk, O Dyer?
You came here thirsting for our blood
Will a lake of it fill your greed, O Dyer?
So many innocents mowed down by you
The Almighty will demand answers, O Dyer.
You scoundrel! Who gave you the right
To make mincemeat of our patriots, O Dyer?
Wreaking terror upon us innocent folk
Did you fancy the taste of power, O Dyer?
Just as you riddled our bodies with bullets
You too will pay the price, O Dyer.
You'll die and head straight to Hell!
Ah! Such torment awaits you there, O Dyer.
Coming face to face on that Judgement Day
What answers do you plan to give, O Dyer?
You Tyrant! Until the end of time you'll be called
The Murderer that you are, O Dyer.
Our Lord will punish you for your crimes
Watch how you get destroyed, O Dyer.
Says Nanak Singh, Which holy book allows
For innocents to be butchered like this, O Dyer?

अंतम फ़तिह

असां वीरां नूं रखणा याद हरदम,
मतां दिउ विसार जमातीआं नूं।
तुसां होवणा नहीं मयूस वीरो,
सीने विच सहारना कातीआं नूं।
जेकर नहीं इतबार ज़बान उते,
आ के वेख लौ छातीआं नूं।
लौ हुण अंत दी फ़तह बुलांवदे हां,
याद रखणा साडीआं बातीआं नूं।

FINAL GOODBYE

Do keep us in your thoughts forever
Your friends you may forget, but your heroes not.
Don't ever despair, if things are bleak
Be ready to die, don't care a jot.
If ever you doubt our word so true
Look at the bullets our bodies got.
'Tis time to bid our final goodbye to you
Just bear in mind, the lesson we taught.

चिठीआं दरदां दीआं, लिख सरकारे पाईआं, चिठीआं दरदां दीआं

शहिनशाह सुन लैण असाडे
दुखी दिलां ने पास तुसाडे
अरज़ां आण सुणाईआं,
चिठीआं दरदां दीआं

रईअत तेरी होई दुखिआरी,
तुध बिन कौण सुणे आहोज़ारी
हिंद विच होण वधाईआं,
चिठीआं दरदां दीआं

रोलट साहिब सी जद आईआ,
रोलट बिल चा पास कराईआ
होर मुसीबतां आईआ,
चिठीआं दरदां दीआं

फिर उडवाईर हुक्म चड़ाईआ,
जिस ने सानूं बहुत सताईआ
कीतीआं वांग कसाईआं,
चिठीआं दरदां दीआं

POSTCARDS OF PAIN TO THE GOVERNMENT SENT OUR POSTCARDS OF PAIN

Please heed our humble pleas, our Lord!
Your hapless folks seek help, our Lord!
And so, we plead in vain,
Our postcards of pain.

Your people face these times so grim
Our cup of sorrow fills to the brim
While the Raj rejoices in its reign,
Our postcards of pain.

Sir Rowlatt came out of the blue,
His Bill got passed, none had a clue
And troubles came like a flood of rain,
Our postcards of pain.

O'Dwyer signed the terrible law,
A heap of misery is all we saw
Only those butchers stood to gain,
Our postcards of pain.

फिर डाईर दी वारी आई,
जिस ने होर मुसीबत पाई
गोलीआं ने चलाईआं,
चिठीआं दरदां दीआं

वीर असाडे चुण चुण मारे,
कौमी लीडर फड लए सारे
कीतीआं ख़ूब सफ़ाईआं,
चिठीआं दरदां दीआं

दस हुण शहिनशाह की करीए,
किहडे ख़ूह विच डुब के मरीए
रब ने मुसीबतां पाईआं,
चिठीआं दरदां दीआं

भरती कर कर वीर पिआरे,
जंग युरप विच भेजे सारे
होईआं जदों लड़ाईआं,
चिठीआं दरदां दीआं

आप दी ख़ातर वीर कुहाए,
हुक्म तुसाडे सदा बजाए
चंगीआं कदरां पाईआं,
चिठीआं दरदां दीआं

And then it was that Dyer's turn
To light a match and let it burn,
Fired bullets at us with such disdain,
Our postcards of pain.

Our brothers killed without a thought,
Our leaders arrested and left to rot,
Fake charges and a smear campaign,
Our postcards of pain.

Tell us our Lord what do we do
Which bottomless well should we jump into
In endless woes we strain,
Our postcards of pain.

Our brothers conscripted, sent off to fight
In Europe's war, to save imperial might
Ah! Those battles so inhumane!
Our postcards of pain.

You asked and we sent our youth to die
Each order followed, no whats or whys
Just look at the rewards we gain,
Our postcards of pain.

बदले उस दे मिलिआ डाईर,
जिस ने आ के कीते फ़ाईर
रब दीआं एहो रज़ाईआं,
चिठीआं दरदां दीआं

कई बेदोशे कैद कराए,
बहुते फ़ांसी पर लटकाए
कर दे जलद रिहाईआं,
चिठीआं दरदां दीआं

शहिनशाह सुण अरज असाडी,
रईअत ड़ाढ़ी दुखी असाडी
देंदी सदा दुहाईआं,
चिठीआं दरदां दीआं

By way of a gift, we got this Dyer
And all he knew was how to fire
So be it, if God ordain,
Our postcards of pain.

Our innocent men sent off to jail,
While hangings go up to a different scale
Please let them free, is our refrain,
Our postcards of pain.

Oh Lord! Do listen to our prayer
Your gentle flock's in utter despair
Their tears flow without restraint,
Our postcards of pain.

THE BAGH, THE BOOK AND OUR BAUJI

Navdeep Suri

It was barely a stone's throw from the small house in Gali Punjab Singh where I was born and spent my first eight years. That infamous red-brick wall of Jallianwala Bagh, unplastered and pockmarked with bullet holes from the Vaisakhi day massacre. Our home was at the far end of one of those narrow alleyways so typical of the old walled city of Amritsar. But getting to the sole entrance into Jallianwala Bagh was a good ten-minute walk through a tight little maze of alleys and by lanes before the final one opened into the main street leading towards the Golden Temple. As a kid often accompanying my mother on her frequent trips to the Golden Temple, I recall hurrying past the Bagh's nondescript wrought iron gate without paying it too much attention.

Every once in a while, some relatives would show up for the customary pilgrimage to the Golden Temple and we would stop over at the Bagh. We would make our way through the gate and down that narrow passage which dramatically opens into a large, enclosed maidan. The pink sandstone memorial stood in front and the footpath took us up to the pockmarked wall – each bullet hole marked as evidence of that terrible day. But for me, the large well to the left of the passage was the place of bad memories. My mother had painted vivid images of helpless men jumping into the well, some to escape the hail of bullets and others after they had been shot. Peering over the ledge into the darkness below, I tried to see if the water was still tinged red with all the blood. There were times when I thought I could hear the screams of the victims echoing dimly as I stood transfixed by the darkness.

Back then, it was an unspoken part of the family folklore that my grandfather – our Bauji – was present in Jallianwala Bagh that fateful day on 13 April 1919. He had gone there for the rally against Rowlatt Act with a couple of friends, we were told. Bauji had collapsed in the stampede triggered by the firing and had been left for dead under a pile of corpses. Both friends died and Bauji himself suffered damage to his hearing in the left ear. He walked out some hours later after regaining consciousness. But this was a subject that he did not want to talk about, and that was that.

Bauji passed away in 1971 in Preetnagar, the tiny village sixteen miles from Amritsar that had intermittently been his home since late 1938. That left our grandmother – the sagacious and effervescent Bhabiji – as the primary custodian of family folklore. She said that during the early years of their marriage, Bauji had spoken of the horrors of that day in Jallianwala Bagh and the trauma that he had suffered. He also told her of *Khooni Vaisakhi*, the book that he had written after the massacre. It was banned by the British government soon after its publication in May 1920 and all copies were confiscated and destroyed. No one in the family had seen a copy of the book and in his later years, Bauji himself showed no inclination to speak about it. Nor did he make any effort to trace it during his own five decades after the book's short-lived existence. He did make a reference to it in his autobiography which was published in 1949. But only in passing. And that was about it.

Or it might have been, but for a couple of remarkable coincidences. Giani Zail Singh, a leading politician from Punjab became India's Minister for Home Affairs in 1980 in the cabinet of Mrs Indira Gandhi. He had previously served as Chief Minister of Punjab and would go on, in 1982, to become the first Sikh President of India. Gianiji was a great fan of Bauji's novels and I have vivid memories of his visit to our home in Amritsar to offer his condolences a few days after Bauji's demise. My father Kulwant Singh – a leading publisher in Punjabi and one who had published many of Bauji's bestselling novels – had been pursuing Gianiji to help in tracing the lost *Khooni Visakhi*. Until now, his efforts had failed to produce any results.

Meanwhile, Dr Kishan Singh Gupta – then a lecturer in Punjabi at DAV College in Hoshiarpur and another fan of Bauji's writings – had stumbled upon an important discovery. His own grandfather was something of a bibliophile and had left behind a treasure trove in their old family home in Muktsar town. The family had packed these away into gunnysacks and they lay in a store for a long while. While rifling through some old boxes in early 1980, he came across an original copy of *Khooni Visakhi* and knew instantly that this was something of historic value – a book that few were aware of, that had not been seen for two generations or more. The book told him something else. Here was Punjabi's foremost novelist writing like an accomplished poet when he was barely twenty-two years old. The discovery prompted Dr Gupta to write a paper titled 'Nanak Singh's *Khooni Vaisakhi*' that was published in the literary magazine *Jagriti* in August 1980. The article was perhaps the first of its kind to focus on Nanak Singh as a poet.

My father, who did not know Dr Gupta, was intrigued by the contents of the article and its detailed references to *Khooni Visakhi*. He reached out to the editor of *Jagriti* to get hold of Dr Gupta's address and excitedly shared the details with my mother Attarjit, who was no stranger to the story. As a veteran Punjabi lecturer in Khalsa College for Women in Amritsar, she was something of an expert on our grandfather's literary corpus. Her Masters' dissertation had focused on the female characters featured in some of his best-known novels and she had written a first-person biography called *Mere Bauji*. The tantalizing possibility of finding the missing Khooni Vaisakhi was equally exciting to her.

And so they went, my mother sitting behind my father on our trusty old Bajaj Chetak scooter, looking for the reclusive Dr Gupta, eventually reaching his place in the heart of the walled city. Within a few weeks, my father was working out arrangements with Dr Gupta to publish *Khooni Visakhi*, complete with a detailed foreword and glossary that he would provide. When I spoke with Dr Gupta about the incident in October 2018 and asked if he would still have the original copy, he went into an emotional explanation about his disenchantment with the Punjabi department for giving insufficient recognition to his scholarship in the language. After he retired from the college, he turned his attention to studying ancient Indian texts on astrology, in which he has now established quite a reputation. In turning away from Punjabi literature, he had also neglected his collection of books and wasn't sure if he would be able to find the original again even if he tried.

In a subsequent conversation, he spoke about *Khooni Vaisakhi* at some length, becoming quite animated as he recalled his excitement on finding the long-lost booklet, writing the essay for *Jagriti* and then working closely with my father to publish the book. He said that he was the one who engaged Gurdial Singh, a typist from Guru Nanak University for the princely sum of fifty rupees to type out the booklet. He proofread the manuscript to make sure that it was free of typos and worked some more on his *Jagriti* essay to make it the preface of the fresh edition of the book.

Meanwhile, a large manila envelope arrived at our home bearing some distinctly official markings. The sender was Ministry of Home Affairs, Government of India, and the OIGS stamp reinforced its official status. Along with a short note from the office of the Home Minister was a sheaf of photocopied A4 papers that carried the full text of *Khooni*

Vaisakhi, but minus the original cover. Gianiji had delivered on his promise to help my father locate the book. We had no idea of where the book was found. Perhaps in some government archive in Delhi, we surmised. Or maybe from the India Office Library in London. The British had the reputation of keeping a record of everything. It would be a delicious irony that they helped us find a book that had been banned by them.

More important, the text of the photocopied pages from Delhi matched perfectly with what Dr Gupta had produced and without much fanfare, my father published *Khooni Vaisakhi* in November 1980 – over six decades after it had been first printed and proscribed! And yet, a small part of the mystery remained. We now had the text of the poem but we had still not seen the book in its original shape. What did it look like? Who had published it? As we approached the centenary of Jallianwala Bagh, I felt that this remained a crucial missing element in the puzzle.

So I decided to call up Kanwaljit chacha – my dad's younger brother in Jalandhar. Within the tight circle of my father's family of five brothers and a sister, he has a well-established reputation as the custodian of all manner of memorabilia related to Bauji – photographs, letters, manuscripts, awards and more. I told him about my project to translate *Khooni Vaisakhi* into English and asked if he had ever come across the original cover of the 1920 edition. His reply caught me by surprise. He hadn't seen the cover himself but had been told about it by one Chetan Singh who had served as Director of the largely forgotten Languages Department Library of Punjabi University in Patiala. Chetan Singh had spent his time at the library digging out old and forgotten works of Punjabi literature and had recently compiled an anthology that featured about seventy of these, including *Khooni Vaisakhi*. Kanwaljit chacha added that Chetan Singh had retired from the job and mostly stayed in his village. But Kulbir chacha – Dad's youngest brother – knew him and if we were lucky, we might be able to get in touch with him.

The next call was to Kulbir chacha. Within hours, he had spoken with Chetan Singh, obtained the title of the book and found out where we could get it and ordered a copy. We could barely contain our excitement as I got the voluminous hardbound copy of his *Puratan Sikh Likhtaan* in my hands, went through the index, opened page 113 and got my first glimpse of the elusive cover. It gave 30 May 1920 as the date of publication, Bhai Nanak Singh Kirpal Singh Booksellers as the publishers and Bhai Nanak Singh of *Satguru Mehma* fame as the author.

Our Bauji

He was quite an extraordinary individual, our Bauji – the man known as Sardar Nanak Singh the Novelist. My earliest memories go back to the time when I was little more than a toddler and he would often come over from Preetnagar village to spend the night at our home in Gali Punjab Singh. I was a bit of a favourite grandchild, I am told, often clambering on to his lap and playing with his flowing beard. I was barely three when Bauji was invited to Delhi to receive the prestigious Sahitya Akademi Award in 1962 from President Dr S. Radhakrishnan. We accompanied him, and my parents have stories of me wandering off on my own into some corridor of Delhi's Vigyan Bhawan before being retrieved by some official and reunited with our anxious entourage.

And as we grew up, some of my most precious childhood memories revolve around the trips to Preetnagar, the sixteen-mile journey from our home mostly done with my parents astride our Chetak scooter. Summer holidays were often spent in the bucolic farmstead amidst the extended family of uncles, aunts, cousins and assorted kids. The joy of outdoor life for city dwellers remains the stuff of nostalgia – climbing trees, chasing chickens, playing kabaddi, khokho and pithoo, walking over to the banks of the canal nearby to savour the juicy little mangoes from Illumdin's famous orchard of yore, pulling out fresh radishes, carrots and turnips over the protests of the neighbours to enjoy some impromptu snacks, and then waiting for the evening.

Amidst all the din and excitement, Bauji had a routine all his own. Once the family had gone to sleep, he would go to his room and start writing, often going on from midnight to dawn. And as the rest of the house started to wake up, he would go to sleep – only to wake up at ten or eleven for a relaxed bath followed by his first meal of the day around noon. This was followed by some reading and possibly another session of writing and a short siesta. A long walk in the evening and a horde of dishevelled kids awaiting his return. An early dinner, followed by a clamour by all of us for a story. This was often the highlight of our day – to have Bauji sit in the middle of a charpoy and some half a dozen of us clustered around Punjab's greatest storyteller.

Nanak Singh with his family

And what a yarn he would weave – of kings and queens, of heroes and villains, of victims and saviours, of good and bad, of right and wrong. The characters so real, the drama so vivid. With expressions changing on the narrator's own face, capturing every twist and turn in the story with a grimace, a smile or a chuckle; breaking spontaneously into a song or verse if the situation demanded. I must have been eight or nine at the time, hanging on to every word, mesmerized by the flow.

It was around that time, or a bit later in 1967 that we left the cramped quarters of the walled city and my father built our new home in Green Avenue, one of the new neighbourhoods being developed at the time by the city council. Dad had become one of Punjabi's leading publishers and his Lok Sahitya Prakashan imprint was much in demand by veteran and also budding writers. The relatively expansive amenities of our new home became a magnet for writers and poets like Shiv Batalvi, Balwant Gargi, Prof. Mohan Singh, Gurmukh Singh Musafir and many others. A room at the front, overlooking the lawn, was reserved for Bauji and became his abode during his frequent visits from Preetnagar. It was also the meeting place for Bollywood personalities like Rajinder Singh Bedi, Balraj Sahni and his son Parikshit when they were filming *Pavitra Paapi* – a popular film based on Bauji's eponymous classic novel. *Pavitra Paapi* was also my first attempt at translation, the outcome being *The Watchmaker* published in 2009 by Penguin India.

Bauji's final sojourn with us was towards the end of 1971, prompted by the outbreak of conflict between India and Pakistan on 3 December. Preetnagar was barely a couple of miles from the border and my father insisted that he and Bhabiji must come to the relative safety of Amritsar. Those were days of air raid sirens and dogfights above our homes, of blacked out windows and a dash to the trenches that we had dug in our backyard. And it now seems a bit surreal that even during that period, some of our friends from the neighbourhood would come over each evening with the hope that Bauji could be persuaded to narrate a story or two. And he seldom disappointed. After almost half a century, a couple of my childhood friends still remember those special times.

The war ended on 17 December with the surrender of 93,000 Pakistani prisoners of war and within days, my grandparents started to insist that they wanted to get back to Preetnagar. The village still looked like an army encampment but they had their way and my father dropped them back in a hired taxi. The sudden vacuum in our home was palpable but the true sense of loss was to come after a mere ten days. Late in the evening of the 28th, we got the dreaded message that Bauji was no more. He had passed away during the night, presumably from a cardiac arrest. He had departed much the way he had lived his life – quietly and with a minimum of fuss, always mindful of those closest to him. I remember crying inconsolably at his cremation, and gazing with a sense of wonder as Chief Minister of Punjab Giani Zail Singh and a host of other important-looking souls arrived for his bhog ceremony a couple of days later. From the vantage point of a twelve-year-old, our loss was personal and it was hard to share it with so many strangers.

Bauji was born on 4 July 1897 in Chak Hamid, a small hamlet in the Daadan Khan tehsil of Jhelum district. Named Hans Raj, he was the oldest of four children born to Bahadur Chand Suri and Lachchmi Devi. His father had a modest trading shop in Peshawar and Hans Raj was barely eight when he was asked to join his father and help with the business. The rest of the family moved a year later, but the joy of a reunion was short-lived. Bahadur Chand died of pneumonia within a year of their arrival, tragically on the same day when his wife was giving birth to his youngest child. At the age of ten, Hans Raj found himself responsible for the family store, an ailing mother and three siblings. Continuing with school was hardly an option. In later years, he was often asked about his formal education and he would smile in response, 'I don't

77

know if I should say fourth grade pass or fifth grade fail. You decide.' It speaks volumes of the sheer genius of the man whose writings would go on to become the subject of over fifty doctoral dissertations.

He stayed in Peshawar for the next ten years or so, developing a passion for music and demonstrating an early talent for stringing rhymes and verses together into rudimentary poetry. An eight-page booklet of his verses was published in 1909 under the title *Seeharfi Hans Raj* when he was all of twelve years old. He showed little appetite for managing the store and was happy to leave it in the more capable hands of his younger brother. Going by his own account in his autobiographical work *Meri Duniya*, his penchant for music and poetry earned him a circle of disreputable friends who sought his company to provide free entertainment at their parties.

He was drifting rudderless until he came under the influence of Giani Bagh Singh, a pious and scholarly figure at the local gurudwara. It was a momentous period for him as he decided to convert to Sikhism. Hans Raj became Nanak Singh in 1915 and embarked with all the zeal of the recent convert to apply his poetic talents towards writing hymns in praise of the Sikh gurus. The most famous of these was *Satguru Mehma*, first published in Amritsar in 1918. It sold over a hundred thousand copies during the next few years and became the bedrock of his financial sustenance as he tried to figure out his true calling. It also earned him the monikers of Nanak Singh 'Kavishar' or poet and of Bhai Nanak Singh – the prefix 'Bhai' being normally reserved for individuals who have made a significant contribution to the Sikh faith. *Khooni Vaisakhi*, in contrast, was a mere blip – written in the aftermath of the Jallianwala Bagh massacre, published in 1920 and lost for the rest of his life. Although we now know that the original edition described the author as 'Bhai Nanak Singh'.

But Jallianwala Bagh did prove to be an important milestone in his life in other ways. He was now a staunch supporter of the nationalist cause and a fervent opponent of British rule. Following the advice of his mentor Giani Bagh Singh, Bauji joined the Guru ka Bagh movement launched by the Akalis in 1922. [*The Akalis were part of a Sikh reformist movement that sought to free the gurudwaras from the control of mahants (caretakers) who were seen as corrupt and dissolute but were friendly to the British. Mahant Sundar Das of the historic Guru ka Bagh gurudwara located in Ghukkevali village about twenty kilometres from Amritsar was a particularly egregious example.*] Bauji was arrested along with a large group of protestors that turned up outside the courts every day to register their protest against Mahant Sundar Das' continued control over land adjacent to the gurudwara. He spent several months in the infamous Borstal Jail in Lahore – a period that he describes as transformational for him as an individual and in his evolution as a writer.

Jail brought him into contact with Pandit Jagan Nath, an influential Congress party activist who had made good use of his influence to bring a trunk-load of books to the jail. The cache included quite a few novels of Munshi Premchand, which Bauji managed to read despite a very rudimentary knowledge of Hindi language and the Devnagiri script. They were to have a defining impact on him as he decided that he had finally discovered his true calling – to write novels that would seek to reform society and make the nation a better place. Enthused by the thought, he started to write his first novel while still in jail – only to have it confiscated and destroyed during a raid on his cell by the prison officials. Spending the severe Punjab winter in a damp cell also meant frequent colds and a complete loss of hearing in the already damaged left ear. His incarceration also had another, rather curious side effect. It became a bit of a sore point in our family and I grew up hearing close relatives lament that Bauji was impractical and perhaps a bit simple-minded when it came to the welfare of his own family. Had he been smarter, they complained, he could have made a very legitimate claim for 'freedom fighter' status and received benefits that his family could have enjoyed.

Bauji emerged from jail as part of the general amnesty to over 5000 prisoners who had been jailed for unlawful protests during the Guru ka Bagh movement. And proceeded to publish *Zakhmi Dil*, his next book of verse. *Zakhmi Dil* used the ingenious device of simple fables to drive home the devious and rapacious nature of the Raj and its persistent efforts to divide and rule. The fables had innocent sounding titles like 'The Traveller and the Djinn', 'The Lion and the Lamb', 'The Cats and the Monkey'. Equally unusual was his use of Urdu in some of the poems that offer a searing account of the brutality with which police forces attacked peaceful Akali protestors at Guru ka Bagh and about the way they were incarcerated. One of these, 'Mind Your Tongue', goes a step further and reminds readers of Dyer and of Jallianwala Bagh if they were to speak out of turn.

The Raj had already showed that it had little tolerance for such 'seditious' literature and, like *Khooni Visakhi*, *Zakhmi Dil* was also banned and confiscated soon after its publication in 1923. In a striking parallel, it was lost to the world for the next several decades and it wasn't until 1990 that my intrepid father found a copy with a dealer of old books. Having previously worked with Dr Gupta, he approached him again for a detailed foreword for the new edition that was published almost seven decades after the original.

Portrait of Nanak Singh in his twenties

The Raj continued to keep a close watch on the media even after the Rowlatt Act was repealed in 1922 and the 1920s clearly weren't an easy time to be a writer, printer or publisher. Printing presses guilty of printing anything tinged with nationalist or patriotic sentiment were deemed 'seditious' and raided by the police. The owners could be jailed for up to three years in addition to being subjected to hefty fines. In *Meri Duniya*, Bauji has an interesting anecdote of his own experience in setting up a printing press in Amritsar soon after his release from jail. He did this with a loan of 3000 rupees from Ram Singh – a childhood friend from his days in Peshawar who would now become his business partner. The business took off but the portfolio included a daily and a bi-weekly that always looked like they might invite the wrath of the government. Other presses had found a neat little solution to the dilemma. Since the owner did not want to risk a jail term, he would get a proxy – usually an unemployed soul willing to sign up as the proxy owner for a monthly salary of about twenty-five rupees.

Bauji was reluctant to follow this route but eventually gave in to relentless pressure from Ram Singh, who argued that the nascent business would collapse if he were sent to jail again. So they found Inder Singh, a young man desperate to earn a few rupees and made him the proxy owner. Barely ten weeks had elapsed and the police was at their doorstep, armed with warrants against the press. The poor soul was sentenced to three years' rigorous imprisonment. Bauji went to see him in jail and was deeply moved by his plight. A heated argument with Ram Singh ensued, but this time

Bauji was not backing down. He sold the press at a loss and handed over the proceeds to Ram Singh with a promissory note that he would refund the remaining amount soon. He also kept his commitment to Inder Singh and continued to pay twenty-five rupees per month to his family for the remaining part of his prison sentence.

The printing press was gone but the desire to write socially relevant novels was burning bright and, in 1924, *Matrayi Maa* received widespread public acclaim as his first novel. After that, there was no turning back and over the next five decades, he pretty much produced a new book every year – mostly novels but occasionally the odd piece of theatre, short stories and even a translation or two. These included *Adh Khidya Phul*, based around the aborted novel that he had started writing in Borstal Jail in 1922 and was eventually published in 1940. I had the privilege of translating it as *A Life Incomplete* in 2012. Another masterly work – *Ik Myan Do Talwaran* revolved around the life of Kartar Singh Sarabha and the Ghadar movement and won the Sahitya Akademi Award. The violence that accompanied the Partition in 1947 shook him to the core and he produced a series of novels including *Agg di Khed* and *Khoon de Sohile* and *Manjdhaar* that delved into its horrors.

Growing up in his shadow, we were largely oblivious of Bauji's fame in the world of Punjabi literature. His books were prescribed texts for anyone studying Punjabi and, every now and then, the association with his name would draw an admiring comment or two from teachers in school, college and university. 'Oh! You are Nanak

Singh's grandson? What a great man! What a fine writer.' But that was all in Amritsar – the city in which I spent my first twenty-two years. Given our long connection with the city, it seemed par for the course. My first jobs took me to Bhilai and Visakhapatnam and, for the first time, I was in places that knew nothing of him – a feeling that was only accentuated during my stints in Cairo and Damascus once I entered the diplomatic life in 1983.

It wasn't until 1996–97 when we were towards the end of our assignment in Washington DC that Bauji unexpectedly came back into our lives as Nanak Singh the Novelist. That was his birth centenary year and in Inder Kumar Gujral, India had its first Punjabi Prime Minister. Gujral was an erudite man and a great fan of Bauji's literary oeuvre. He took it upon himself to ensure that the centenary was celebrated in a big way, with a major event at the Prime Minister's official residence at 7 Race Course Road where he released a postage stamp and first day cover featuring Bauji. Extensive coverage in the Punjabi media also carried the occasional reference to my position in DC. As word travelled to the US, I was faintly bemused by suddenly finding myself much in demand at events organized by the Punjabi diaspora in Washington, Chicago and San Francisco to celebrate Bauji's legacy and literary heritage. Having grown up taking it for granted, I found myself humbled by the sight of hundreds of well-settled members of our community who spoke passionately of the impact of his novels during their own formative years, of ladies who swore that they learnt to read Punjabi due to the passion fired by his books. I, as a mid-level diplomat at the embassy, was being feted for no reason other than the fact of being Nanak Singh's grandson. It was much the same during our assignment in London and an important element in the decision to finally give in to my mother's entreaties and start work on translating *Pavitra Paapi*.

The Bagh

As denizens of Amritsar, we also took Jallianwala Bagh for granted. It was just there, and unlike the Golden Temple next door, it did not attract vast crowds of the religiously inclined, nor the hordes that descended on festivals and special days. Even the Flame of Liberty memorial in the Bagh eventually came up in 1951, a good three decades after this lament in *Khooni Vaisakhi*:

No plaque, no bust, no monument
To mark the place we died, O friends?

And when it did come up, it too was just there, not asking for any attention and staying largely forgotten. Just as we had forgotten that caustic reminder from the martyrs in *Khooni Vaisakhi*:

Make time to visit this Bagh of ours
And hear our gallant souls, O friends.
With heavy heart, they mock our nation
Thanks so much for your love, O friends!

Even in our own case, I must confess that the Bagh had slipped from our consciousness. It was the powerful scenes of the massacre and the Hunter Commission of Inquiry scene in Richard Attenborough's *Gandhi* that painfully jogged the memory. They reminded, albeit briefly, of the connect that we were losing with our own history. That point was driven home again during a recent visit to Amritsar. A dinner time conversation with some old friends revealed a rather foggy picture that mixed Brig. Gen. Dyer with Lt. Governor Michael O'Dwyer and showed a distinctly patchy recall of the Rowlatt Act and the broader context in which the protests and the massacre took place.

For that reason alone, there is merit in providing a clearer snapshot and timeline which will enable the lay reader to place the poem in a more accurate historical framework. This matters because *Khooni Vaisakhi* is more than just a poem or a work of literature. It is also an important contemporaneous account that reflects events, emotions and sentiments during that tumultuous first fortnight of April 1919.

Much of the Punjab was already seething with resentment well before April 1919. The Great War which lasted from 1914 to 1918 had taken a terrible toll on the state that had contributed disproportionately to the war effort. According to one learned estimate, at the start of the war Punjabi soldiers comprised as much as two-thirds of the Indian army's cavalry, 87% of the artillery and 45% of the infantry. During the four years of the war, Punjab contributed a further 450,000 soldiers to the Indian army. As the war dragged on and British forces suffered setbacks in Mesopotamia in 1916, the demands for more recruits kept growing. The Commonwealth War Graves Commission estimates that the size of the Indian army grew near ten-fold from 150,000 to 1.4 million during the four-year period and over one million of these were deployed overseas. More than 74,000 died fighting a war that wasn't theirs, to defend an imperial order that had subjugated their own nation. The tombstones in France and Germany, in Turkey and Greece, in Iraq and Palestine, in Tanzania and Singapore bear eloquent testimony to the terrible human cost that the war inflicted on Indian soldiers – a majority of them from the Punjab. Even the British army recognized the valour and sacrifice of Indian soldiers in serving the empire, a fact reflected in the 9,200 decorations and eleven Victoria Crosses awarded to them.

The Raj largely administered the Punjab with the support of large feudal landlords and they were often provided with a mix of incentives and quotas to push able-bodied young men towards the recruitment camps. Although coercion was rampant, many also joined the army willingly due to the obvious attractions of a decent salary and pension and the more intangible factor of *izzat* or respect that was imbued by a uniform. But by early 1918, there were clear signs of fatigue and weariness in the peasant communities. Reports that tens of thousands had died fighting unknown enemies in alien climatic conditions and distant lands without getting a proper cremation or burial also fed into the resentment.

From his vantage point as a veteran ICS officer at Government House in Lahore, Lt. Governor Michael O'Dwyer was privy to these sentiments and recognized that the Raj's most prolific source of recruits had been wrung dry. Based on his advice, the government decided to suspend fresh recruitment for a period of ten weeks starting 31 March 2018. But the reprieve was short-lived. A German offensive and fresh Allied losses on the Western Front prompted a quick reversal and the suspension was lifted on 13 April. It is estimated that between April and October 1918, a further 77,000 men were mobilized from Punjab. There is ample evidence of unethical practices and coercion being deployed during this last round with tehsildars given specific recruitment targets for the villages under their charge. Bauji's *Ik Myan Do Talwaran* also speaks at some length about the anger and resentment caused by these actions.

The plunder of young men from rural areas was aggravated by the devastation caused by the plague of 1915 and its debilitating aftermath. To make matters worse, there was a flu epidemic in Punjab and the monsoons also failed in 1918, leading to poor harvests and a steep increase in food prices. The public was suffering but the sweeping powers given to the administration under the Defense of India Act of 1915 virtually outlawed any form of dissent or protest.

As the Great War drew to a close, there was an expectation that the imperial government would honour its promise of carrying out meaningful economic and political reforms that would ameliorate the hardships and also foster greater local participation in governance. Instead, it used the pretext of the Ghadar movement and other limited disturbances to appoint a Sedition Committee headed by Justice Sir Sidney Rowlatt in December 2018. Their report produced the Anarchical and Revolutionary Crimes Acts – popularly known as the two Rowlatt Bills – that were placed before the legislature in February, passed by the Imperial Legislative Council in Delhi on 10 March and became law on 21 March, 1919. The Rowlatt Act allowed the government to continue with emergency measures enacted in the wartime Defense of India Act, including preventive detention, arrest without warrant, in camera trials and strict controls on the press. Dubbed 'No Dalil, No Vakil, No Appeal', the passage of the Act prompted the resignation of prominent nominated Indian members of the Legislative Council including Madan Mohan Malviya and Mohammed Ali Jinnah. For the people of Punjab, it was the last straw.

Meanwhile, Mohandas Karamchand Gandhi had returned to India in January 2015 after spending twenty-one years in South Africa. While in Johannesburg, he had come up with the ingenious concept of satyagraha to register the Indian community's first organized protest against racial discrimination in 1906. I was India's Consul General in Johannesburg in 2006 and helped in recreating the march from the venue of the historic Empire Theatre to commemorate the centenary of the first satyagraha. Prominent ANC leaders like Kgalema Motlanthe (later Interim President of South Africa) and Ahmed Kathrada (a close associate of Nelson Mandela who was also a co-conspirator in the Rivonia Trial and spent twenty-seven years with Mandela on the Robben Island prison) joined us in the march.

Gandhi was concerned about the potential impact of the Rowlatt Act and tried to prevent the bills from being passed. He met the Viceroy Lord Chelmsford on 4 March and again sent him a telegram on 12 March saying, 'Even at this eleventh hour, I respectfully ask his Excellency and his Government to pause and consider before passing the Rowlatt bills.'

Following the bill's passage, Gandhi decided to launch a satyagraha campaign and called for a nationwide hartal for 6 April. It was to be a day of prayer, to be launched from Chowpatty Beach in Bombay. It was a big success and there was widespread support for hartal in Bombay, Ahmedabad, Lahore, Calcutta, Puri, Madras.

Amritsar reported a near total hartal that day, the campaign being actively coordinated by Saifuddin Kitchlew and Dr Satyapal – two of the city's leading members of the Indian National Congress. Kitchlew was a thirty-one-year-old Muslim barrister who was educated in Cambridge and Germany, and had established a flourishing practice in Jalandhar after his return to India. He was an articulate, energetic and able organizer who reportedly moved to Amritsar after having difficulties with the Deputy Commissioner of Jalandhar. Dr Satyapal was a little older, a respected surgeon and an active supporter of causes dear to the city's Hindu community. Together, they put up a show of Hindu–Muslim unity that caught the attention of the British administration and lay observers alike. In his *The Life of General Dyer* published in 1929, biographer Ian Colvin writes of the spectacle of Hindus and Muslims drinking out of the same water vessels at Amritsar and worries that it is 'a breach of caste ... strange, ominous, unprecedented.'

Alarmed by the developments, Miles Irving, then Deputy Commissioner of Amritsar, wrote to the Commissioner of Lahore Division on 8 April expressing very grave concern over the situation and asking that a 'really strong force will have to be brought in and we shall have to be ready to try conclusions to the end to see who governs Amritsar.' The events in Amritsar also prompted Gandhi to board a train for Delhi on 8 April en route to his first visit to Punjab. But the Raj did not want him anywhere near Punjab. He was arrested at Mohammed station near Palwal and served orders prohibiting him from entering Delhi or Punjab.

Ram Navami, the spring festival celebrating the birth of Lord Rama, fell on 9 April and was traditionally celebrated with large processions running through the major thoroughfares of Amritsar. Led by Kitchlew and Satyapal, the spirit of communal amity was once again striking and caught the unfavourable attention of the rulers – especially since Kitchlew and Satypal continued to agitate against the Rowlatt Act. Irving was quizzed during the Hunter Commission Inquiry about the communal harmony at display during the Ram Navmi celebrations. He replied, 'I saw that they were using religious organizations to serve political ends, which always in the long run means mischief.' On the specific question that 'Hindus were drinking water touched by Muhammadans and were joining the religious procession', Irving reiterates that the motives underlying the unity had a 'sinister purpose'. The administration had had enough and later that afternoon, Lieutenant Governor O'Dwyer issued orders for the removal of the leaders of the 'virulent agitation'. The duo were arrested on the morning of 10 April along with two other local leaders and deported by road to Dharamsala.

Historians regard the arrest of Kitchlew and Satyapal as a blunder that triggered the horrifying events which unfolded over the next few days. News of their arrest spread like wildfire and by noon on 10 April, sizeable crowds had started to gather in Hall Bazaar with the objective of reaching Deputy Commissioner Irving's office and giving him a petition for the release of the leaders. This involved crossing the Railway Carriage overbridge that linked the walled city with the civil lines area. Determined to prevent the protesters from crossing the bridge at any cost, the administration sent an armed force that soon started firing to disperse the crowd. Around thirty people were killed and a number of others wounded, forcing the protestors to carry the dead and wounded and retreat from the bridge. Angered by the wanton violence unleashed on unarmed protestors, a section of the leaderless crowd went on a rampage through Hall Bazaar, burning down the Town Hall building and attacking several banks and government offices. Five Europeans were killed and three others severely injured, including Marcia Sherwood – a missionary who worked as Superintendent at the Amritsar Mission School – who was cycling back from work. She was rescued by some Hindu shopkeepers who gave her medical treatment and kept her safe until she could return. Louis Fischer, in his biography of Gandhi, supports the view that 'banishing of the leaders from Amritsar removed the two men who might have restrained the populace'.

Following an understanding with the Deputy Commissioner's office that the size of the funeral procession would not exceed two thousand and that the last rites would be completed by two p.m., the dead were taken to the Sultanwind area on the morning of 11 April for burials and cremations. The funerals passed off peacefully but it was clear that the city administration had lost its nerve. A.J.W. Kitchen, a senior ICS official who was Commissioner of the Lahore Division was sent to take charge of the situation and he quickly declared the need for decisive action to restore the prestige of the Raj. Despite the relative calm in the city, he left for Lahore and after consulting Lieutenant Governor O'Dwyer, he wrote to Major General William Beynon asking the army to take charge of the security situation and requested for an officer who was not afraid to act. He had his prayers answered in the form of Brig. Gen. Dyer, commander of the cantonment at Jalandhar. Dyer reached Amritsar late in the evening and took charge of the city. In the process, the civil administration of the city effectively abdicated its own responsibility and became a silent spectator to the carnage that followed.

With the army in sole command, Dyer established a temporary camp in the Ram Bagh gardens a short distance from the walled city. On the morning of 12 April, he led a strong patrol through sections of the city as a show of force.

Dyer carried out another patrol through the city on the morning of 13 April, this time accompanied by proclamations that were read out to the public. They stated that any gathering of more than four people would be treated as unlawful and liable to dispersal by use of force; that no resident would be allowed to leave the city without a permit; and that a curfew would come into force from eight p.m. with orders to shoot violators. British accounts suggest that he encountered a sullen and hostile populace and the city's resentful residents booed at the troops from their rooftops as the patrol made its way through the narrow lanes. Small groups of young men jeered at the soldiers and shouted slogans in support of Gandhi and Dr Kitchlew and a few of the more aggressive ones even spat in the direction of Dyer. He returned seething to Ram Bagh around one-thirty p.m. and heard a little later that crowds were beginning to assemble in Jallianwala Bagh in open defiance of his orders.

At Jallianwala Bagh, associates of Kitchlew and Satyapal had arrived early to establish a stage from which the nationalists could make their speeches. As crowds of people started to stream in, they merged with the thousands who were already present for Vaisakhi – an important day in the local calendar that celebrates the Hindu and Sikh new year, the harvest season and the founding of the Khalsa faith by Guru Gobind Singh in 1689. It is a day when people traditionally come to Amritsar from neighbouring towns and villages to celebrate the festival at the Golden Temple. Estimates of the total size of the crowd present when Dyer arrived on the scene vary – from a high of 20,000 in the Congress report to around 10,000 to 20,000 per the Hunter report. Various accounts indicate that the speakers included local nationalists like Brij Gopi Nath, a bank employee and part time poet; Durga Das, a journalist with *Waqt* newspaper;

Abdul Majid, Hans Raj, Gurbax Rai and others. Historian V.N. Datta writes that Durga Das took the stage and called for two resolutions – repeal of the Rowlatt Act and release of Kitchlew and Satyapal. Others were in the process of delivering speeches and reciting patriotic poems when Dyer made his infamous entry.

Leading a force of twenty-five Baluch and twenty-five Gurkha troops armed with Lee Enfield .303 rifles, two armoured cars with mounted Vickers machine guns and another forty Gurkhas armed only with khukhris, Dyer arrived at the Bagh at around four-thirty p.m. The armoured cars couldn't make it through the narrow entrance and had to be left outside along with the khukhri-wielding Gurkhas. The remaining fifty entered and took positions. Dyer gave them the order to start firing within thirty seconds of their entry. No warnings were issued and the firing continued for ten minutes – the troops repeatedly reloading their guns and firing until they had almost exhausted their stock of ammunition. A total of 1650 rounds were fired, creating mayhem as unarmed civilians ran towards the five-foot-high wall at the rear of the Bagh and attempted to scale it. Dyer directed the soldiers to fire towards the wall, creating carnage, with bodies of the dead and the wounded falling in a heap that was four or five deep at some places. Some sought safety behind the makeshift stage and the small samadhi on one side, while others ducked behind the embankment of the well. Quite a few fell into the well as they tried to escape the bullets, while others lost their lives in the stampede that ensued. With its main entrance blocked by the troops and limited options available to escape, the Bagh became Dyer's killing field.

The slaughter lasted barely ten minutes but the sheer number of casualties in that brief span paint a stark picture. The Hunter report, with good reason to play down the casualties, estimated a total of 379 killed and 1200 wounded. Other official estimates indicated 400–500 dead, while the Congress inquiry report places the figure closer to 1000. The plaque at the Bagh itself speaks of the grounds being 'saturated with the blood of about two thousand martyrs' – a figure that probably includes both the dead and the wounded.

In his recent book on Gandhi, historian Ramchandra Guha provides an unusual perspective into the massacre through the diaries of J.P. Thompson, then Chief Secretary of Punjab. Thompson writes that at a party – yes, a party – at Governor's House on 14 April, he met G.A. Wathen, Principal of Khalsa College Amritsar, who told him that in Jallianwala Bagh, 'The troops shot men like rabbits as they ran,' adding that, 'The only thing that can save the situation was that L.G. (Michael O'Dwyer) should disown the action taken.' Thompson himself takes the view that although 'it seems to have been a bloody business, 200-300 killed in a garden ... probably it will be justified by result.'

During the century since the massacre, much has been written about Dyer's personality, his mindset, his motives and the larger political context in which he gave the fateful order to fire. He was born in Shimla in the family of a brewer, studied at Bishop Cotton School and was fluent in Hindustani. Having joined the military, he had a fairly undistinguished career, rising to the position of Colonel before being given the temporary rank of Brigadier General and command of the cantonment in Jalandhar. Around fifty and not in the best of health, he often took recourse to alcohol to dull the pain caused by an early onset of arteriosclerosis. There appears to be little doubt that the act was premeditated, that Dyer went to the Bagh with the full intention of teaching the nationalists a lesson and to instill fear about the might of the Raj in the hearts and minds of the masses. He also wanted to avenge the death of the five Europeans on 10 April – an ambition equally shared by Kitchen and Irving. His own words in the Hunter report provide ample evidence about his intent. 'I fired and continued to fire until the crowd dispersed, and I consider this is the least amount of firing which would produce the necessary moral and widespread effect ... from a military point of view not only on those who were present but more specially throughout Punjab. There could be no question of undue severity.'

Writing in *An Autobiography* in 1936, Jawaharlal Nehru provides a fascinating first-hand insight into Dyer's mindset. He travelled from Amritsar to Delhi in a night train and when he entered the compartment, most of the passengers were asleep. He occupied a vacant upper berth and went to sleep. When he woke up in the morning, he discovered that the other fellow passengers were all British military officers and among them was Dyer, 'holding forth in an aggressive and triumphant tone' about 'how he had the whole town at his mercy and he had felt like reducing the rebellious city to a heap of ashes, but he took pity on it and refrained.'

The complete absence of empathy for the victims was also manifest in the fact that neither Dyer nor Irving deigned to visit the Bagh in the aftermath of the massacre. Testimony published in the Congress report provides heart-rending details of the injured crying out for water, of women coming in search of their husbands and children, of survivors defying the eight p.m. curfew to return to the Bagh with pitchers of water, of doctors risking punishment as they treated hundreds of bullet wounds, of unclaimed bodies rotting in the harsh April sun as vultures gathered overhead.

But Amritsar's agony did not end at Khooni Vaisakhi. Based on the recommendation of O'Dwyer, the Viceroy Lord Chelmsford issued a Martial Law ordinance on 14 April, giving Dyer and others like him the latitude to mete out a set of outrageous punishments with the singular objective of teaching the natives a lesson. Perhaps the most egregious of these euphemistically termed 'fancy punishments' was the infamous 'crawling order' that was imposed by Dyer in the Kaurianwali Gali, also known as Kucha Kurishan. This was the 150-metre long lane where Marcia Sherwood had been assaulted, a place that Dyer now pronounced sacred. He decreed that any Indian passing between the two police pickets placed at either end of the street would have to crawl on all fours. British soldiers were on hand to photograph the humiliation and to kick those whose buttocks got raised from the ground as they attempted to reach their homes. For the hundreds of families living on the crowded street – many of them reputed and affluent merchants – the trauma was beyond description. Others endured whipping and flogging on the slightest pretext and hundreds of others were subjected to torture and incarceration in the name of identifying those involved in killing the five Europeans. Water and electricity were cut off for days and collective punishment of the worst kind was imposed on a prosperous city of 1,50,000.

Amritsar, of course, wasn't the only place in Punjab that suffered from the excesses of martial law. Lahore, Lyallpur, Kasur, Gujrat and other cities suffered their own share of indignities that have been documented in some detail by Helen Fein in her book *Imperial Crime and Punishment.* These included asking students to attend several roll calls in a day, banning two or more persons from walking abreast, prohibiting the use of bicycles, asking offenders to recite poems in praise of martial law, saluting British officers, touching the ground with the forehead by way of salaam and whatever else the sahibs thought fit. But perhaps the most heinous act in the aftermath of Khooni Vaisakhi was the use of aircraft to drop bombs and strafe unarmed civilian protestors in Gujranwala town on 14 April.

Meanwhile, the Martial Law and Rowlatt Act restrictions tried to make sure that whatever happened in Punjab stayed within Punjab and it took several weeks before the rest of the country got an inkling of the reign of terror spanning the land of five rivers. As Nehru wrote in *An Autobiography*, 'The Punjab was isolated, cut off from the rest of India; a thick veil seemed to cover it and hide it from outside eyes. There was hardly any news, and people could not go there or come out of there … Odd individuals, who managed to escape from that inferno, were so terror struck that they could give no account. Helplessly and impotently, we, who were outside, waited for scraps of news and bitterness filled our hearts.'

Outrage over the blatant abuses carried out in the name of martial law grew as the first reports started to trickle in. Sir Rabindranath Tagore, already famous as India's first Nobel laureate and knighted by the British in 1915, took the momentous decision to renounce his knighthood. In a letter that he wrote to Lord Chelmsford on 31 May 1919, he said, 'The enormity of the measures taken by the Government in the Punjab for quelling some local disturbances has, with a rude shock, revealed to our minds the helplessness of our position as British subjects in India ... The accounts of the insults and sufferings by our brothers in Punjab have trickled through the gagged silence, reaching every corner of India, and the universal agony of indignation roused in the hearts of our people has been ignored by our rulers ... The time has come when badges of honour make our shame glaring in the incongruous context of humiliation, and I for my part wish to stand, shorn of all special distinctions, by the side of those of my countrymen, who, for their so-called insignificance, are liable to suffer degradation not fit for human beings.'

As Ramchandra Guha says, Jallianwala Bagh was to have a profound impact on Gandhi's own evolution as a leader of India's freedom struggle. Having been thwarted in April, he eventually made his first visit to the Punjab in June 1919, coming to Lahore on the 24th and to Amritsar a week later. He arrived at the station to a rousing welcome, spent a few days and came back a few months later for the inquiry report instituted by the Indian National Congress. He travelled extensively in the Punjab in November–December and stayed on until the end of the year to attend the annual meeting of the Congress, chaired by Motilal Nehru and held in Amritsar for symbolic and political reasons.

The whitewash of Jallianwala Bagh attempted by the European majority on the Hunter Commission contrasted so blatantly with the testimony that Gandhi and his team had collected from some 1700 witnesses that his faith in the British sense of fairness was irredeemably damaged. He decided that a new movement of protests was the only way to make the Raj see reason and proceeded to outline a blueprint of his non-cooperation movement. As Guha says, Jallianwala Bagh and the brutality with which the subsequent martial law was enforced in Punjab 'transformed him from an Empire loyalist to an implacable opponent of British rule.'

Martial Law in Punjab was lifted in August 1919 and Rowlatt Act was eventually repealed in March 1922, a full three years after it came into force. But by that time, the damage was done. Jallianwala Bagh and the Khooni Vaisakhi of 1919 marked a pivotal moment in the fortunes of the British Empire and its Jewel in the Crown. Only a few years earlier in 1911, King George V had laid the foundation stone of the new imperial capital in New Delhi. Construction work on the world's last imperial capital was in full swing to get the Viceroy's palace and other major public buildings completed, when Jallianwala Bagh happened. But the moral authority of the Raj had been grievously damaged. Led by stalwarts like Gandhi, the nationalist movement gathered steam and by the time the capital was inaugurated in 1931, the empire had started to lose its aura of invincibility. A mere sixteen years later, India's independence was a reality and the sun had finally set on the empire.

Of the principal characters, Dyer died a sad and lonely man in a small cottage in Somerset on 23 July 1927. He suffered from arteriosclerosis and spent his last years in ill health, still haunted by the censure he had faced in the Hunter report and the consequent decision to strip him of his temporary rank of Brigadier General and revert him to Colonel. His biographer Nigel Collett writes in *The Butcher of Amritsar* that, 'There was no memorial stone made to Dyer and no resting place for his ashes. Annie (his wife) destroyed all his papers. She was careful not to leave anything behind. The great-grandchildren today hardly have any effects or photographs or any living memory of Reginald Dyer. Annie wanted the memory to be gradually forgotten.'

Lt. Governor Michael O'Dwyer fared much better in terms of his reputation, being largely let off by the Hunter report. He claimed that he could not be held responsible because the army was in effective control. Despite his close involvement with the imposition of martial law and the excesses that took place under his watch, Conservatives in London regarded him as the 'saviour of Punjab' for his decisive actions in quelling the disturbances. This was unpalatable to Udham Singh, a twenty-year-old who was present in Jallianwala Bagh and survived the massacre. He waited for twenty-one years before getting the opportunity to fire two bullets from a hidden pistol and assassinate O'Dwyer on 13 March 1940 at Caxton Hall in London. Having accomplished his mission, Udham Singh surrendered to the police and used his trial to explain, 'I did it because I had a grudge against him. He deserved it. He was the real culprit. He wanted to crush the spirit of my people, so I have crushed him ... I am not scared of death ... I have seen my people starving in India under the British rule ... What greater honour could be bestowed on me than death for the sake of my motherland.'

Udham Singh was convicted and hanged to death in July 1940 at the Pentonville Prison in north London. But it wasn't until 1974 that his remains were exhumed and brought back following the persistent efforts of Sadhu Singh Thind, a legislator from Kapurthala. He accompanied the remains back to India and the martyr was cremated near his birth place in Sunam. A portion of his ashes are preserved in a sealed urn that, befittingly, lies in Jallianwala Bagh.

Nanak Singh receiving the Sahitya Akademi Award from President Dr S. Radhakrishnan

Bauji would have been a couple of years older than Udham Singh at the time and it is unlikely that the two survivors ever met. Udham Singh joined the revolutionary movement, coming close to Bhagat Singh and working to overthrow the British government through armed struggle. Bauji chose a pen instead of a gun to vent his feelings. *Khooni Vaisakhi* is both a work of literature and contemporaneous history that provides an unusually vivid insight into that tumultuous first half of April 1919. It also sets the tone for some of his other work to inspire the freedom movement.

THE SINS OF THE GREAT–GRANDFATHER
Justin Rowlatt

I wasn't expecting to react as strongly as I did when I visited Jallianwala Bagh, the walled garden where the 1919 Amritsar massacre took place. I certainly wasn't expecting to cry.

I'd imagined I'd struggle to connect with the horror, that it would seem abstract; an episode from a distant history. But even after ninety-eight years, the garden is resonant with its memory. When you see the bullet holes that pock the walls, or peer into the well where so many died, you can't help but imagine the terror the protestors must have felt.

My tears hijacked me when the time came to say goodbye to Mr Mukherji. As chairman of the Jallianwala Bagh board, Sukumar Mukherji – 'SK' – is in charge of the garden. He had very kindly given me a personal tour and, as I thanked him for his hospitality, my voice faltered and I began to weep.

He didn't seem surprised. Apparently, it is common for Indians and Britishers alike, to be overcome by emotion when they visit the site. But I have more reason than most to feel ashamed and humbled by what happened at the Bagh.

That's because the demonstrators who were killed by British troops had gathered there to protest against a repressive law inspired by and named after my great-grandfather. I am talking about the infamous Rowlatt Act.

The passage of what Gandhi called the 'Black Act' led directly to the events at Amritsar on 13 April 1919.

It was a truly draconian piece of legislation. The law suspended the most basic of civil liberties for those suspected of plotting against the Empire. It provided for stricter control of the press, allowed the authorities to arrest anyone who seemed suspicious to them without warrants, permitted indefinite detention without trial. You could be imprisoned for up to two years simply for running a 'seditious' newspaper. That is why thousands of Indians gathered in Jallianwala Bagh that day: urged by Gandhi, they were there to express their disgust and fury at the legislation my great-grandfather, Sidney Rowlatt, had authored.

My link to this dreadful episode had been very much on my mind when I came to live in India with my wife and four children in February 2015. I was worried that my family name would make us targets for any lingering anger. It might also make it hard for me to do my job: wouldn't being a scion of an emblem of imperial evil be a handicap in my new role as the BBC's South Asia correspondent?

A century on, it is worth remembering just how appalling what happened at Amritsar was.

S.K. Mukherji had led me along the route the commander of British forces, Brigadier General Reginald Dyer, took with his ninety troops. Like me, Mr Mukherji has direct family connection to the events. His grandfather, Sashti Charan Mukherji, had been in Jallianwala Bagh on the day of the massacre. He had told his grandson how the troops marched in through the narrow entrance and then formed into two semicircles, blocking the only exit. He saw them bring their rifles to their shoulders and aim out at the crowd. Then, without warning, they opened fire. Sashti managed to duck behind a stage that sheltered him from the hail of bullets. They maintained the fusillade for ten minutes.

According to the imperial record they fired 1,650 rounds and killed 379 people. At least 1,137 people were injured.

Indian sources put the numbers far higher.

SK showed me the well into which terrified people had dived for cover. 120 bodies were recovered from it. As we turned back to the garden, Mr Mukherji recalled his grandfather telling him how, their ammunition now almost exhausted, the General had ordered his troops to pack up and leave. The wounded were left writhing in agony on the ground. Dyer ordered a curfew, threatening to shoot any Indian seen out on the streets.

The Amritsar massacre was a turning point in Indian history. In his book *English History 1914-1945*, the historian A.J.P. Taylor called it 'the decisive moment when Indians were alienated from British rule'. Mahatma Gandhi, then a relatively marginal figure among India's nationalist leaders, launched his first 'satyagraha' – campaign of non-violence – in protest at the Rowlatt Act. According to the course book used by tens of millions of Indian high school students, 'it was the Rowlatt Satyagraha that made Gandhiji into a truly *national* leader [original italics].'

After I'd wiped away my tears and recovered my composure, SK and I weaved our way back through the crowds of Indian schoolchildren. I told him I was astonished that he appeared to feel no animosity towards me. 'You feel shame, so I feel no anger towards you,' he said.

I walked back slowly to my hotel through the crowded streets, trying to work out how I felt about what I had seen and experienced in the garden.

SK is right about shame, I reflected. I feel deeply ashamed of my connection to this appalling episode. A Sikh in a bright yellow turban sailed serenely by on a bicycle. But do I – should I – feel in any way responsible?

Sir Sidney Rowlatt died long before I was born. In the one sepia-tinged picture I have of him he is a figure from another age, an elderly and rather rakish-looking Edwardian gentleman.

The best account I've read of how he came to play his inadvertent role in Indian history is from Patrick French's magnificent history of the independence movement, *Liberty or Death: India's Journey to Independence and Division*. Mr French does not mince his words. 'Sir Sidney Rowlatt is one of the forgotten anti-heroes of India's struggle for freedom. He was a comparatively insignificant judge with a fiscal bent', he writes, whose appointment in India came 'by chance'.

His dismissive summary is tempered by the quote he includes from *The Dictionary of National Biography*. It reveals that Sir Sidney's 'classical scholarship, although restrained by an essentially modest nature, could, when the occasion demanded, produce elegant, impromptu Latin verse.'

So why was my classically-minded great-grandfather in India?

As Patrick French says, he was a judge, specializing in commercial law. He'd built his career in London. He'd never visited India but, towards the end of the First World War, he was appointed head of a committee tasked with investigating the causes of, what was to the British authorities, a very worrying upsurge in revolutionary activity in Britain's Indian dominions.

This new pattern of unrest had begun towards the end of the nineteenth century. The climax was an attack on the then Viceroy himself: Lord Hardinge. It happened just before Christmas 1912. Viceroy Hardinge had just arrived at Delhi railway station to inaugurate the construction of the new city. He clambered aboard an enormous elephant.

I'll let Patrick French take up the story.

'Sitting in an elaborate silver Howdah, he advanced slowly down Chandni Chowk' – the main thoroughfare of what we now call Old Delhi.

'His Excellency had not got far,' says French, 'when his helmet shot into the air, a bang was heard six miles away, and the servant holding the State Umbrella was blown to pieces. Hardinge subsequently remembered noticing some yellow powder on his elephant, and feeling "as though somebody had hit me very hard in the back and poured boiling water over me". An unknown Indian had hurled a bomb at the living symbol of imperial power. One of the Viceregal eardrums burst, and it was to take many years for all the nails, screws and gramophone needles to work their way out of his body.'

Rather bizarrely, the bomber, who was never caught, had packed his weapon with rusty gramophone needles as shrapnel.

This was just one of a host of acts of what would now be called terrorism. Indeed, a key reason the British were shifting their capital from Calcutta to Delhi was because the violence had become so hard to contain. 'Seditionists' – as the opponents of the colonial authorities were dubbed – were tossing bombs all around, assassinating or, more usually, attempting to assassinate, high officials, and generally disrupting the smooth running of the imperial machine. There had even been bomb attacks in London.

There were fears that Britain's enemies were helping foment unrest. This is real *The Riddle of the Sands* stuff: international espionage. The Germans were believed to be funding Indian independence activists and other subversive organizations. The effort had spilled into Afghanistan where, in 1915, a German diplomatic mission had tried to persuade the Amir to declare full independence from Britain, enter World War on the side of the Central Powers, and attack India.

There were suspicions that Bolshevik agitators were also spreading discontent and distributing cash.

British anxieties were heightened by the Easter Rising in Dublin in 1916 and then – more frightening still – the Russian revolution in 1917.

Which is where my great-grandfather comes in. The British government wanted a proper reckoning of what was happening in India and what should be done about it.

Sidney Rowlatt was chosen to head what became known as the 'Sedition Committee' and, in late November 1917, he set sail from Plymouth to Bombay in a convoy escorted by half a dozen destroyers.

My uncle Richard has collected together the letters Sir Sidney wrote to his wife during his visit to India. I was hoping they might give an insight into his thinking as he travelled around India gathering evidence for his report. But my great-grandfather was a dutiful public servant. He is an engaging correspondent, describing the extraordinary things he sees and experiences on his journey, but the letters barely mention his real purpose in India.

His most revealing comment comes late in his trip. It was early April 1918 and he had just arrived in Delhi. The new city hadn't been built yet. George V had announced at the 1911 Delhi Durbar that the British authorities were to move the capital from Calcutta to Delhi and had laid the foundation stone of what was to become New Delhi. But the First World War intervened and, when my great-grandfather turned up there, very little building work had been done.

Here's what he wrote. 'We had driven out to see New Delhi where they are going to build a vast official city with a Viceregal Lodge to which Buckingham Palace will be a cottage – residencies & offices for all the government – houses for native chiefs &c &c. It covers a square mile or two at least & has a "processional road" as long as the Long Walk at Windsor. There have been 7 cities at Delhi & all have perished with the folk that built them – the ruins are all here

– & here we go & build an 8th just when our show is tottering! However it was a very jolly afternoon.'

So that's how my great-grandfather saw his job, he was there help shore up the Raj just when – as he privately acknowledges – the show was 'tottering'.

I've got a wonderful tattered old copy of the report that my great-grandfather's committee produced. It contains a meticulous account of all sorts of seditious activities; murders, shootings, bombings – hundreds of them – and shows how difficult they were for the courts to tackle: witnesses were intimidated and judges and lawyers were attacked and murdered.

But there is a fascinating and crucial omission. There is no discussion of the rights and wrongs of the cause that was driving this agitation: the demand of many Indians for self-rule and independence.

This troubles me deeply. Sir Sidney clearly knew the game was already up for the British in India yet does not to explore whether there might be a better way to defuse the tensions in the country than repression.

He will have known what a huge contribution Indian soldiers were making to the allied efforts in the Great War. Around 1.3 million Indians fought for the British, over 74,000 were killed. He will have almost certainly also have been aware that, in recognition of this sacrifice, some very modest moves towards self-government were planned for what was to become the Government of India Act of 1919. So why didn't he use the evidence he had gathered to suggest these go deeper, as so many Indians were demanding?

My guess is that Sir Sidney will have regarded speculation about constitutional matters as outside his remit. His failure – and that of the authorities in London – to appreciate how his legislation would be received by the Indian public explains why my great-grandfather's efforts to stabilize British India failed so signally.

Intriguingly, there is a hint in the letters that he had a pretty clear idea of just how toxic his recommendations would prove to be. It is January 1918 and Sir Sidney is on the train from Bombay to Calcutta. He is boyishly excited to discover he has an entire carriage to himself: 'really a sort of small saloon' with 'a perfectly comfortable couch to sprawl on'.

'To complete my splendour', he continues, 'one of the Governor's attendants, in a khaki & red uniform, a fine red turban & the monogram & coronet of the Governor embroidered on his chest is travelling in a neighbouring compartment as my servant as far as Calcutta.'

He describes watching the magnificent scenery roll by and later how, in the dining car, he gets into conversation with two Englishmen 'of good position'.

'By the way, I think they guessed my errand,' he reveals to his wife in that evening's letter. 'On leaving, I gave them my card & said I expected they'd hear my name & that I should be lucky if they didn't – meaning that I expected to be well abused before I left India.'

This indicates that not only did my great-grandfather already have a fairly good idea what the conclusions of his report were likely to be, but also the opprobrium they were likely to generate.

If so, he was right. His report and the legislation that followed proved to be one of the key stimulants in mobilizing mass opposition to colonial rule.

The first evidence of the strength of feeling came in India's Central Legislative Council as the Viceroy, Lord Chelmsford, attempted to ensure the Sedition Bill was passed. It was based on repressive legislation brought in during the war as a temporary effort to control enemy activity in the country. When the same measures had been put before the Council in 1915, the twenty-two elected Indian members had happily voted them through. But what was acceptable in wartime was not in peace and when what became dubbed the Rowlatt Bill came before the Council in 1919 there was a wholesale revolt. Every single Indian member opposed it. The legislation only passed with the support of the thirty-four other British-appointed nominees whose job it was to ensure that whatever London wanted, it got.

Muhammed Ali Jinnah, the prominent Muslim leader, articulated the anger of the Indian members most forcefully. There was 'no precedent or parallel in the legal history of any civilized country to the enactment of such laws', Jinnah declared, in a letter to Viceroy Lord Chelmsford. When the Bill was passed into law in March 1919, he resigned from the Imperial Legislative Council on the grounds that 'the constitutional rights of the people have been violated', and that the legislation, 'ruthlessly trampled upon the principles for which Great Britain avowedly fought the war".

The Rowlatt Act and its repercussions were very much in my mind as I started work in the Delhi Bureau of the BBC. I did not feel responsible or see how anyone could hold me responsible for something, however heinous, done by an ancestor three generations earlier. However, my fear was that many Indians would disagree. In that I was proved spectacularly wrong.

My name was never a problem. I was occasionally teased for my unfortunate family history, but I never experienced anger, nor even disapproval. Indeed, if anything Indians seem to warm to me because of my connection to their country. I would often puzzle over why this might be. I wasn't certain my compatriots would be so generous to the relative of an Indian who had been instrumental in prompting the slaughter of hundreds of British people.

In the end, the most powerful explanation came from Mahatma Gandhi's grandson, Tushar Gandhi. I expected some hostility when we met one hot afternoon in July 2017 at the gracious New Delhi mansion where his grandfather had been assassinated in January 1948. Instead, he offered me gratitude in the form of a magnificently backhanded compliment.

'I appreciate your great-grandfather's role to provide the first nail in the coffin of the Empire,' Tushar said with a laugh as we shook hands in the garden.

We stood in the shade of a small tree as he explained why the Act that took my great-grandfather's name was so important to the Mahatma. 'The beauty of the Rowlatt Act was that he didn't have to be a spin doctor to make people understand that it was unjust,' he said. 'It was so transparently malicious in intent that he could use it to create anger, to create resentment but then channel it towards the kind of protest he wanted it to be – a peaceful protest.'

And, Tushar believes, it is the fact that the Indian opposition to the British was non-violent that is the key to understanding why there is not more resentment and anger between the two nations. 'It allowed us to believe we had won independence,' he explained. 'And it let the British console themselves by saying, "We were benevolent by giving them independence."'

It's a seductive argument for a relative of Sir Sidney Rowlatt. Yes, the legislation was repellent but it had positive – if wholly unintended – consequences.

That said, it doesn't assuage my sense of shame.

I still believe the measures my great-grandfather's committee recommended were unjust and misguided. I still find the omission of any discussion of the justice of the independence cause shocking. I still am sick to my stomach at the way the British forces behaved in Jallianwala Bagh. And I am also still appalled that my great-grandfather was honoured for his work on the Sedition Committee with a Knighthood.

Currently based in London, Justin Rowlatt was the BBC's South Asia correspondent based in New Delhi until the summer of 2018.

KHOONI VAISAKHI: A HISTORICAL AND HUMANISTIC PERSPECTIVE

H.S. Bhatia

The contribution of S. Nanak Singh to the history of modern Punjabi literature stands out as that of a trailblazing writer. Possessing an exceptional sensibility, he explored and executed his literary understanding across several genres and left behind a variegated oeuvre, even though his image is that of the father of the Punjabi novel. His contemporaries, as well as generations of writers who came after him have, without fail, acknowledged his influence over their works. His own life experiences often shaped his writing, and thus he could liberate the Punjabi reader from the shackles of religious and communal thinking. By using the tropes of romance as well as tragedy in his writings, he was able to touch the hearts of his readers. His books became immensely popular and it would not be an exaggeration to say that he was the first writer to bring a book to the hands of the Punjabis. Many a reader learned the Gurmukhi script and the Punjabi language in order to read his books.

Nanak Singh believed in writing as a vehicle for resistance and through his writings, he wanted to liberate his reader from all kinds of insularity and to inculcate empathy in them.

Some critics describe the lack of sentimentality as a weakness in his fiction and critically comment on his projection of a middle-class, reformative ideology. They also point out that although he handled the redemption of his characters plausibly, the genesis of the extenuating circumstances and the need to change them was beyond either his understanding or control. Despite all this critical commentary, no critic has ever been able to deny the importance of his contribution. Dr Harbhajan Singh's comment in *Nanak Singh Abhinandan Granth* seems very relevant in this context:

> The Punjabi readers have immensely enjoyed the fiction of Nanak Singh even though they have not critically analyzed it. In my opinion it is a good thing. In Punjabi literature, there is many a writer who has been analyzed but not enjoyed or relished.

I

Nanak Singh's career as a novelist began with *Matrayi Ma* (1924) and ended with *Gagan Damama Bajeya* (1967). During this long span, he created some three dozen novels. For his novel *Ik Myan Do Talwaran* (1960), the Sahitya Akademi honoured him in 1961 with the President's Award. However, long before he formally entered the world of fiction, he had already earned laurels in the realm of poetry. Beginning with the *Seeharfi Hans Raj* (1909), he went on to create memorable poems like *Satguru Mahima* (1918), *Gur Kirat* (1919), *Khooni Vaisakhi* (1920) and *Zakhmi Dil* (1923). As a playwright, he published his play *B.A. Pass* in 1944, even though it had been staged many a time for the previous two years. We come to know this, from his own words, as recorded in the complete collection of his plays (2012): 'After this [*B.A. Pass*], I wrote, from time to time, many a drama and one-act plays, like *Ware Gandh, Chaur Chanan, Parhaku di Vauhti Desi Sharab, Char sau Veeh, Beruzgari, Shaikh Chilli, Kharpainch, Dhobi da Kutta* and the like and also had them staged.' Similarly his autobiography, *Meri Duniya* (1949), appeared at the time when he was deeply involved in the creation of his fictional world. Apart from these, his short stories, essays and translations have also been largely neglected.

II

Nanak Singh was born in a poor Hindu family in the town of Jehlum (now in Pakistan) and was named Hans Raj. Coming under the influence of Sikhism, he changed his name from Hans Raj to Nanak Singh. Poverty prevented him from getting formal education. However, he had an immense desire, almost a passion, to learn and as a result, life itself opened up like a beautiful book for him to browse through. He started composing poetry and soon earned the title of 'Nikchu Shair' (young poet) from his friends. In his autobiography, he records that it was with this early practice in rhyming verses that he made his entry into the realm of literature:

How do I find you those verses juicy
With salty blood, my tongue is dripping!
Lucky folks like you won't understand
Through a man's eyes, his life is dripping.

119

Just ask the miserable ones out there
The earth and sky, both are dripping.
Says Hans, don't ask about our hapless fate
'cause where I sleep, the roof is dripping.

In 1918, he wrote *Satguru Mahima*, a poem occupied with the adulation for the Sikh Guru. This composition marked a shift in his writing: from recounting individual pain and suffering, he veered towards religious reformation. *Satguru Mahima* became very popular and started to be counted among the hymns, and although no one regarded Nanak Singh as the eleventh guru, his words were revered as much as the scriptures. Apart from earning him respect, the work also reduced to a considerable extent his economic worries. The widespread sale of millions of copies of *Satguru Mahima* also prepared a large and dedicated reading public who waited eagerly for his next creation. However, his literary sensibilities were to undergo yet another drastic change.

III

It was the era of colonial rule in India. The British Raj used the policy of 'divide and rule' because of which Sikhs, Hindus and Muslims were divided into sects. Movements like the Singh-Sabha and the Arya Samaj were doing valuable work by awakening consciousness and sowing the seeds of freedom in the public, but at the same time they were generating a sense of religious disharmony. During this time, Punjabi literature flourished under the hands of Bhai Veer Singh, Bhai Mohan Singh Vaid, S. Charan Singh Shaheed, Dhani Ram Chatrik, and Puran Singh, and with works like Bhai Veer Singh's epic poem *Rana Surat Singh* (1905), Dhani Ram Chatrik's *Bharthari Hari* (1905) and *Nal Damayanti* (1906). Puran Singh's *Khule Maidaan* (1922) and *Khule Ghund* (1923) had not yet been composed.

The tone of Bhai Veer Singh's epic was primarily that of mysticism. In the unfolding of the mystery of life and death, there was no room for political or social ruminations. Long before the publication of *Chandanwari* (1931), even Dhani Ram Chatrik was involved in exploring the mythical and Puranic heritage of the Hindu religion. It was largely due to the Ghadar movement, Calcutta's Kavi Kutya, the massacre at Jallianwala Bagh, the Gurudwara Reform and Akali movements that a religious, nationalistic and confrontationist kind of poetry came into being. Poets like Hira Singh Dard (1887–1965), Gurmukh Singh Musafir (1899–1976), Vidhata Singh Teer (1901–1973), Darshan Singh Awara (1906–1982), and Firoz Din Sharaf (1898–1955), came to perform on the stage during that era. Out of them, Hira Singh Dard, Vidhata Singh Teer and Firoz Din Sharaf responded fiercely to the Jallianwala Bagh massacre. Hira Singh Dard's poetry dealt with religious thought, the principle of equality and a craving for freedom. The first part of his composition, *Dard Sunehe*, was published in 1920, whereas part two and part three were published in the years 1921 and 1923 respectively. Portraying the pain, he wrote:

Angry guns poured out a rain of bullets
Yet an air of spring to the Bagh it brought.

His raging fire burnt every thing in sight
Yet a garden bloomed in that dusty plot.
He wanted to finish my name forever
Yet a memorial eternal is what we got.

Similarly, Vidhata Singh Teer's book *Teer Tarang* (1926) described the pain and suffering in his poem 'Ralaya Khoon Hindu Musalman Aiethe'.

Ah! As I start to write this tragic tale,
My pen weeps and pleads in protest.
They wanted just to serve their nation
Instead, laid down their lives right here.
Hugging each other tight, they left this world
Lies mingled the blood of Hindus and Muslims here.

By describing the macabre scenes of the massacre, he was trying to encourage the spirit of brotherhood amongst people. He reflected on nature to portray the poignancy of the times:

'Twas the height of savagery and oppression
Nod the garden's flowers in silent assent.
Every inch of land wails out in pain
Each plant and tree cries for justice here.
Bullets rained merciless on our innocent men
Lies mingled the blood of Hindus and Muslims here.

The massacre became a turning point in the history of Indian independence. It naturally became the motif in many poetic renderings, many of which were held at the Jallianwala Bagh. Like in the aforementioned poem of Vidhata Singh Teer, Firoz Din Sharaf also portrayed his pain in a poem which was recited at a gathering in Jallianwala Bagh on 23 June 1923. Sharaf included this poem in his anthology *Dukhaan de keerne*, the mention of which seems very relevant here:

Even the brutal rule of Nadir Shah eclipsed
By harshness of laws framed by the English here.
I just can't find the words to tell
Of the terror unleashed on our people here.
To make things worse, O'Dwyer sent that wire
Letting Dyer give orders to fire right here.

Sacrificed like goats our Indian brothers
At the hands of butchers cruel right here.
Some crying in pain and others sobbing
Wailing as they waited for death right here.
Like flailing fish lay the thirsty wounded
While streams of blood flowed around them here.
Look deep and you find them all the same
Rahim, Kartar and Bhagwan are all here.
Zamzam and the Ganga merged together as one
Lies mingled the blood of Hindus and Muslims here.

Mohamad Hussain Arshd Amritsari also expressed anguish at the massacre. The British Government banned not only S. Nanak Singh's *Khooni Vaisakhi*, but also *Teer Tarang* by Vidhata Singh Teer and Firoz Din Sharaf's *Dukhaan de keerne*.

It becomes quite clear from this that the pressure of these poems and the public approbation of and reaction to them, was powerful enough to disturb the British government so much as to lead it to issue such orders.

IV

After *Satguru Mahima*, Nanak Singh liberated his poetic sensibility from the themes of romance and tragedy. He engaged with the immediate events of the times, the Jallianwala Bagh massacre therefore proved to be the most important landmark. While going through *Khooni Vaisakhi*, one gets the impression that just as Guru Nanak Dev did not hesitate in speaking the truth when he described the officials of the time as 'Raje Shinh Mukadam Kutte' (the kings act like lions and the officials like their dogs), and just as Shah Mohamed portrayed the pain of the Punjabis after the defeat of the Sikhs at the hands of the British, Nanak Singh walked along the same path of rebellion and confrontation. Just as Shah Mohamed explored the deep-rooted psyche of Punjab and rejected sectarian and separatist thoughts, Nanak Singh also spoke from the stand point of Hindu–Sikh unity. If we consider Shah Mohamed a historical poet, then we have to acknowledge that Nanak Singh's poem is a historical artefact and, as a part of Indian literature, it should be conserved with much care.

Nanak Singh starts the poem with an invocation, as was tradition. However, instead of praying to the deity for success, Nanak Singh invokes Guru Gobind Singh, who had taken up the sword to fight oppression after all efforts at peaceful settlement had failed. The writer thinks that he could use his pen to fight Raj. After the invocation, the poem starts with 'Rowlatt Bill da Raula', and describes the frustration among common people caused by the passing of the 'black law', which entailed that anyone could be jailed or put under house arrest indefinitely without trial.

Consequently, the poem very systematically recounts the entire history of the times: all that took place before that fateful day, which led to the order by Dyer to open fire on the public. With the sequential narrative of all the crucial events that surrounded the massacre and by recording the responses of the public to each event, the poem can also be seen as a reliable source for historians, just as *Heer* by Waris Shah is considered by historians to be a good source of historical facts of eighteenth-century Punjab. What makes the poem truly remarkable is the way in which Nanak Singh balanced the facts while keeping to the poetic form and tone.

Within the framework of *Khooni Vaisakhi*, there is a clash between two opposing elements: one side is represented by the common people, who wanted to live a peaceful life and are roused to gain freedom for their country. The other side is the powerful British government that wanted to exploit and loot the country with the help of armaments.

However, just as during the war from 1839–1846 between Punjabis and the British, some Punjabis adopted the course of desertion rather than fighting the British, in this case also instead of fighting the oppressive government, they resorted to becoming informers for the regime and betraying the people of India. Nanak Singh described such people in his words:

> But a scene so different on the other side
> Friends gather at homes to celebrate.
> A mission accomplished, the Act is done
> 'Tis time for wine and feast ornate.
> Their quislings, turncoats and traitors all
> Come laden with gossip and tales narrate.

However, ultimately, the poem becomes a picture of a public which has risen above divisions of religion and caste and is expressing its united opposition to the foreign rulers. The composition acquires the shape of a complete creation because his own experience had been woven into his poetic consciousness. In his autobiography, *Meri Duniya*, Singh has written, 'My society and I – my humanity and my self – are so much in consonance that I can never ever think anything apart from them. If anything hurts my society or my humanity it hurts me.'

translated from the Punjabi by Gajinder Bagga
poem excerpts translated by Navdeep Suri

Harbhajan Singh Bhatia is the former dean of languages at Guru Nanak Dev University, Amritsar. Gajinder Bagga is the former head of the postgraduate department of English at Khalsa College, Amritsar.

ACKNOWLEDGEMENTS

I have been privileged to receive the support and advice of some truly remarkable individuals during the journey of this publication. My father Kulwant Singh Suri, who is close to eighty-seven years, found a new burst of energy as he embarked on this project with me. He put me in touch with Professor Harbhajan Singh Bhatia and Dr Kishan Singh Gupta, even as he took it upon himself to publish a revised and expanded Punjabi edition of *Khooni Vaisakhi* for the centenary of Jallianwala Bagh. My mother Attarjit Suri donned her academic hat to provide valuable guidance in interpreting some of the more complex linguistic challenges I encountered in the text. My wife and eternal companion Mani offered her advice on all important aspects of the book. My friend Satyasheel added a dash of his poetic sensibility to the project.

I am grateful to Prof. Bhatia, for his deep insights into the genre of protest poetry that was prevalent in the 1920s, and for placing *Khooni Vaisakhi* squarely in the context of India's freedom struggle. I'm also grateful to Prof. Gajinder Bagga for translating Prof. Bhatia's essay into English.

I deeply appreciate the spontaneity with which Justin Rowlatt agreed to contribute a very personal perspective in his beautifully sensitive essay, 'The Sins of the Great-grandfather'.

As a family, we remain indebted to Dr Gupta for helping us find *Khooni Vaisakhi* after sixty long years, and for his remarkable work highlighting Nanak Singh's felicity as a poet.

And it has been a pleasure working with the HarperCollins team. I found myself in sync with poetry editor Sohini Basak from our very first conversation; art director Bonita Shimray has been creative in imagining the cover design, and publisher Udayan Mitra has provided all the encouragement and support that I needed when he declared *Khooni Vaisakhi* as a rare publication.